FAMILY

C000072433

on tl

ISLE

OF

WIGHT

Laurence Main

Scarthin Books, Cromford, Derbyshire   1992

FAMILY WALKS
ON THE ISLE OF WIGHT

Family Walks Series
General Editor: Norman Taylor

THE COUNTRY CODE
Guard against all risk of fire
Fasten all gates
Keep dogs under proper control
Keep to paths across farm land
Avoid damaging fences, hedges and walls
Leave no litter
Safeguard water supplies
Make no unnecessary noise
Protect wildlife, wild plants and trees
Go carefully along country roads
Respect the life of the countryside

Published 1992.

Phototypesetting, printing by Higham Press Ltd., Shirland, Derbyshire

ISBN 0 907758 56 8

BEWARE THE BLACK GANG!

1

Preface

In an age of fast travel over long distances, it is so easy to forget the simple pleasure of walking the ancient footpaths. Yet there is no better way of really getting to know an area. A week spent exploring the Isle of Wight along its waymarked rights of way can be more satisfying than an expensive trip around the world. This tiny but enchanted island is a prime example of how much better it is to visit a place so that you can really feel you know it, rather than skim over it. The Island has set a high standard in maintaining its paths and really welcomes the pedestrian tourist. Couple this with the abundance of attractions to visit and the excellent public transport and there can hardly be a better place for a family walking holiday.

~~~~~~~~

Acknowledgements

There were many anonymous people who made my trips to the Island a real pleasure. British Rail ticket collectors, bus drivers, shopkeepers and ordinary people in the street, all had time to help and a natural charm which made the short trip across the Solent seem like a visit to a different, more courteous, age. All types of accommodation abound on the Island. I can vouch for the helpful, tolerant and hospitable spirits of the youth hostel wardens. For various reasons, I couldn't make the trips for this book with my children, which is why they don't feature in the photographs. They did make several visits during school holidays with their grandmother, however, to follow in my footsteps.

About the author

Laurence Main was born in Oxford, leaving the city with a degree from its university to teach for six years in Swindon. The Isle of Wight was a place for trips, especially before taking the night boat from Southampton or Portsmouth to France (his wife, Paule, is French - they have four children, two boys and two girls, born between 1976 and 1990). The family moved to Dinas Mawddwy in Gwynedd when Laurence was working as the Assistant Secretary and Education Officer of the Vegan Society Ltd. He is the voluntary footpaths secretary for the Ramblers' Association in Meirionnydd. Since 1987, he has been a full-time writer of footpath guides and contributes regularly to walking magazines. He has three other titles in the Family Walks series, covering Mid Wales, Snowdonia and Oxfordshire.

2

CONTENTS

MAP OF THE AREA

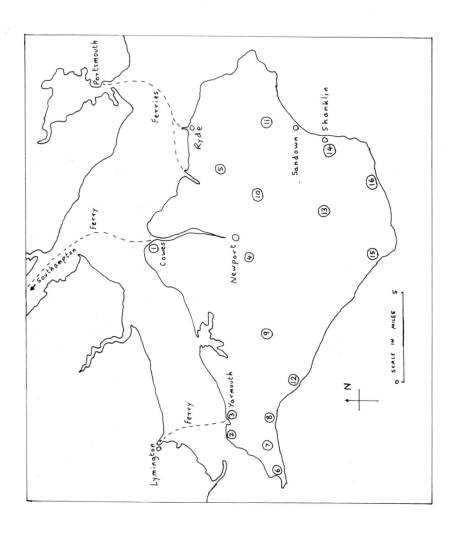

Introduction

The Isle of Wight is an ideal place for a family walking holiday. If you are carrying an infant in a papoose or have very young, or very old, legs, then this is the book for you. None of the walks reach four miles in length, but each is packed with interest. Allowing time for toddlers to explore and for attractions to be visited, they give satisfying half-days, while a beach is never far away. Most walks can be linked together easily, either by a short walk or a ride on a bus or train. Conveniently, just one Ordnance Survey Outdoor Leisure map (No. 29) is needed for the whole island. This and the bus timetable can be your key to wider examination of this enchanted Island. Here, though, are maps at a generous scale which mark the stiles, gates and signposts which give the learner so much confidence. If you are new to walking, you could hardly choose a better place to visit than the Isle of Wight. There are over 500 miles of rights of way here and they are treated as valuable assets by the local population of around 130,000 and those who attract and cater for the one and a half million holidaymakers who take the ferry, catamaran, hydrofoil or hovercraft across the Solent each year.

The Needles, Alum and Freshwater Bays, Blackgang Chine and Cowes are all celebrated in childhood memories of seaside holidays. They are all on a diverse coastline which runs to over 60 miles and is followed by a highly recommended long distance Coastal Path. This can be walked with the aid of County Council leaflets or Alan Charles' excellent guidebook (published by Thornhill Press). The County Council have also promoted several trails which would give an adult a good day's walking. These reveal that the Island is the microcosm within the macrocosm of southern England. The interesting geology is reflected in the contrasting landscapes. Roughly diamond in shape, the Isle of Wight is about 23 miles from west to east. A massive belt of chalk occupies this line, with the vast white cliffs at The Needles in the west and Culver Cliff in the east displaying its depth. Chalk also forms the highest point of the Island (787 feet) at St. Boniface Down above Ventnor and St. Catherine's Down (775 feet) above Blackgang. A deeper bed of sandrock forms the Undercliff. Cutting between north and south, where the maximum distance is only 13 miles, brings a sequence of clay and sand. Wight only became an island when the chalk ridge linking it with Dorset was broken about 8000 years ago. Coastal erosion is still very active, so great care must be taken on all clifftop walks.

Visitors have always come to the Island. One theory is that the Roman name Vectis refers to Ictis, where the Phoenicians and Greeks traded for tin with the Ancient Britons. The Solent may have been fordable then, while Southampton was the market for Cornish tin as late as the 15th century. King Charles I was isolated here before his execution, while smugglers made the 'Back of Wight' (southern coast) notorious in the 18th and 19th centuries. Queen Victoria lived in Osborne House and brought respectability to the Island. Her poet laureate, Alfred Tennyson, chose to live in its romantic western end, below Tennyson Down. The Island's vitality and sense of freedom also attracted Keats, Swinburne, Dickens and Priestley. Yes, there are 'quaint' touristy villages and centres such as Sandown, Ryde, Newport and Cowes are full of people, but even in the height of the summer season it's easy to find solitude or, at least, kindred spirits, by taking a few steps along the public footpaths. Come out of season and even the popular tourist centres are depopulated. A few attractions, such as the Wax Museum at Brading, are open even on Christmas Day. Most can cater for a half term holiday in late October. Whenever you come, you won't need to invest in expensive gear. Sandown and Shanklin are regularly recorded as the sunniest resorts in England.

MODEL CRICKETERS AT GODSHILL

6

ON THE WAY TO NODES BEACON

Symbols used on the route maps

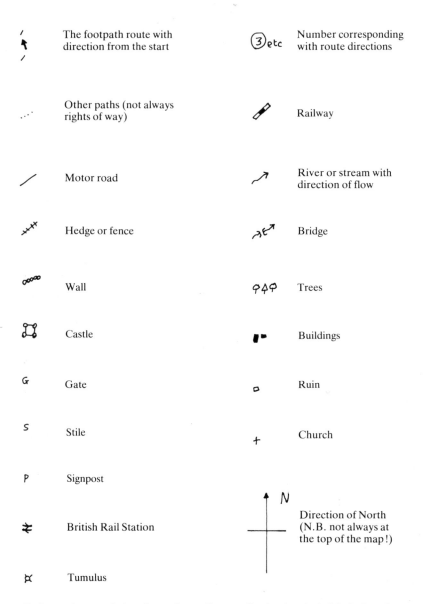

The footpath route with direction from the start

Number corresponding with route directions

Other paths (not always rights of way)

Railway

Motor road

River or stream with direction of flow

Hedge or fence

Bridge

Wall

Trees

Castle

Buildings

Gate

Ruin

Stile

Church

Signpost

British Rail Station

Direction of North (N.B. not always at the top of the map!)

Tumulus

Each map has a scale in miles and a gradient profile showing the height in feet above sea level and the distance in miles from the start.

8

Cowes

Outline Carvel Lane Bus Terminus ~ Tourist Information Centre ~ The Parade ~ Egypt Point ~ Northwood House ~ Maritime Museum ~ Chain Ferry ~ Carvel Lane Bus Terminus.

Summary Cowes is famous for its yachting clubs and 'Week'. This walk takes you along the seafront before climbing up to Northwood House. It then visits the Maritime Museum and the Chain Ferry before returning to the start of the walk.

Attractions The urban pavements and park paths of Cowes are one of the highlights of the Island, especially during the international yachting festival known as Cowes Week in early August. This northern tip of the Island looks toward the Solent and is crammed with boatbuilding yards, ferry landings and yacht clubs. Amongst them is the Vectis Tavern, one of the oldest pubs on the Island and a regular flood-victim. Uffa Fox, the sailor and yacht designer who used to entertain Prince Philip during Cowes Week, lived at No. 83 in the High Street (The Prospect - now a museum). Next door are the offices of the Royal Ocean Racing Club. When you reach the Parade, notice the shelter on your left. A plaque commemorates the sailing of the 'Ark' and the 'Dove' in 1633 to establish the colony of Maryland. Here, too, the Polish destroyer Blyskawica ('Lightning') assisted in the defence of the town during an air-raid on the night of 4th/5th May, 1942. The hub of Cowes Week is the Royal Yacht Squadron Clubhouse. Parts of this building were a coastal fort built by Henry VIII. The row of small cannon outside it were originally on William IV's yacht 'Royal Adelaide'. Now they are fired to start and finish the yacht races. A delightful walk between Princes Green and the sea leads to a small automatic lighthouse at Egypt Point. Albert Ketelbey, the composer of 'In a Monastery Garden' once lived nearby. An anti-submarine boom stretched from here to the mainland during World War II and was opened only at secret times to allow British and Allied ships to pass.

Turning back into Cowes, Beaulieu House is passed on your right. Napoleon III and his Empress Eugenie stayed here in 1872. The railway engineer George Stephenson lived in a mansion nearby and gave Princes Green to the town. Visit the churchyard of Holy Trinity to see pieces of the Fastnet Rock forming a memorial to the yachtsmen who lost their lives in the 1979 Race. Peaceful paths through Northwood Park lead to Northwood House. This was designed by Nash for the Ward family in
continued on page 12

9

Route 1

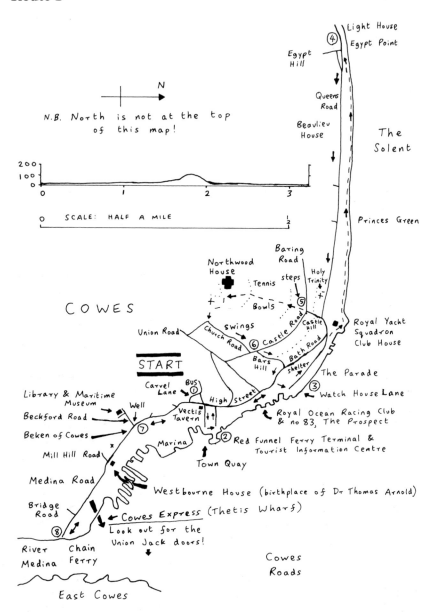

N

N.B. North is not at the top of this map!

200
100
0

0   1   2   3

0   SCALE: HALF A MILE   ½

Light House
④ Egypt Point
Egypt Hill

Queens Road

Beaulieu House

The Solent

Princes Green

Baring Road
Northwood House
Tennis   steps   Holy Trinity
COWES
Bowls   ⑤
Union Road   swings   Castle Road   Castle Hill   Royal Yacht Squadron Club House
Church Road   ⑥ Castle Road   Bath Road
START   Bars Hill   shelter   The Parade
Carvel Lane   Bus ①   ③ Watch House Lane
Library & Maritime Museum   Well   High Street   Royal Ocean Racing Club & no 83, The Prospect
Beckford Road   Vectis Tavern
Beken of Cowes   ⑦   Marina   ② Red Funnel Ferry Terminal & Tourist Information Centre
Mill Hill Road
Medina Road   Town Quay
Bridge Road   Westbourne House (birthplace of Dr Thomas Arnold)
⑧   Cowes Express (Thetis Wharf)
River   Chain   Look out for the Union Jack doors!
Medina   Ferry   Cowes Roads

East Cowes

Route 1

Cowes

3¼ miles

START   *The bus terminus in Carvel Lane, not far inland from the Red Funnel Ferry Terminal and the Tourist Information Centre (G.R. 496961).*

ROUTE

1. *Go down Carvel Lane to the High Street. Turn left along it. Pass the Vectis Tavern and turn right along the Town Quay. Go left to the Tourist Information Centre.*

2. *Walk inland by the Fountain Arcade and go right along the High Street. Pass No. 83 (Uffa Fox's house, The Prospect) and the Royal Ocean Racing Club on your right. Turn right down Watch House Lane.*

3. *Turn left to walk along The Parade, with the sea on your right. Notice the shelter on your left. Continue along the coastal path, passing the cannons of the Royal Yacht Squadron Club House. Go ahead to the Light House at Egypt Point.*

4. *Turn sharply left to return along Queens Road, with the sea now on your left. Pass Bealieu House on your right, then Holy Trinity Church. Turn right up Castle Hill.*

5. *Go ahead up the steps to Northwood Park. Reach Northwood House, go left to St. Mary's Church and turn right through its graveyard to Church Road. Go left downhill.*

6. *Turn left along Castle Road, then right down Bars Hill to Bath Road. Go right to return to the High Street. Continue past the West Cowes Marina, on your left, to the restored Town Well on your right.*

7. *Take the next road on your right, Beckford Road, to reach the Library and Maritime Museum on the corner of Westhill Road on your left. Retrace your steps to what is now Birmingham Road and turn right along it, then down Medina Road to the Chain Ferry.*

8. *Turn round to walk back to Carvel Lane. Notice the Union Jack doors across the estuary on your right. Admire the yachting photographs in the window of Beken of Cowes on your left.*

Public Transport   Carvel Lane, Cowes, is the terminus for buses Nos. 1, 1A (both from Ryde via Newport), 2 (from Sandown via Shanklin and Newport) and 3 (from Sandown via Newport). Red Funnel Ferries provide services between Cowes and either Southampton or Portsmouth. The Chain Ferry between Cowes and East Cowes crosses the River Medina at frequent intervals during the day. The Cowes Express ferry to Southampton leaves from Thetis Wharf.

1837. Given by them to the town, it is the scene of grand balls during Cowes Week. Nash also designed the tower of St. Mary's Church.

Descending to the sea again, pass the West Cowes Marina. The restored Town Well is also passed as you divert to the Maritime Museum which is housed in the library. Admission is free and the opening hours are from 9.30 a.m. to 6 p.m. Mondays-Fridays and 9.30 a.m. to 4 p.m. on Saturdays. Many of the models came from John Samuel White, the firm that built warships in nearby yards. When you reach the Chain Ferry, you could cross the Medina on this floating bridge before turning back the way you came. Even if you stay on dry land, there are views to be had across the river to the doors of the British Hovercraft Corporation. These were painted to form a Union Jack to celebrate the Queen's Jubilee in 1977. Retained by popular request, this is where the first successful hovercraft (the SRN 1) came into the world on 30th May, 1959. Notice Westbourne House on your right. Dr. Thomas Arnold, the headmaster of Rugby School, was born here on 13th June, 1795. Look out, too, for the window of Beken's, on your left. This is world famous for its yachting photographs.

Refreshments   Plenty of choice in Cowes!

WALKING THE COASTAL PATH

12

Fort Victoria

Outline   Fort Victoria ∼ Coastal Path ∼ Monks Lane ∼ Norton ∼ Fort Victoria.

Summary   Fort Victoria is now set in a Country Park. This route leads out of the trees along a lane and inland field paths before returning to the coastal fort.

Attractions   The old fort is one of several built to guard the Island's coastline and the access to the naval dockyard at Portsmouth. There was a blockhouse here in the 16th century, replaced by a battery during the Napoleonic Wars. With relations with France still tense, the fort was built in 1852-53. Triangular in shape, it stands on top of the old battery. Much of the landward side has now been demolished, but the main armament was housed in the two seaward faces, with a further gun at the apex of the triangle. A detachment of the volunteer Isle of Wight Artillery Militia was the first to garrison the fort, in July, 1855. This was because the regular army was fighting in the Crimea. The fort was built too close to sea level and soon became outdated. By 1876 it was ripe for demolition. Instead, it became a barracks for the Royal Artillery. They removed their guns and handed it over to the Royal Engineers in 1891 and Fort Victoria became the base from which coastal minefields were laid to defend the Needles Passage. To transport the mines a light railway was constructed, a length of which can still be seen adjacent to the cafeteria. Searchlights were also tested here. The Royal Engineers also helped to rescue a great number of the crew of H.M.S. Gladiator, a cruiser weighing 5,750 tons with a complement of 250 men. In bad weather on 25th April, 1908, she collided with the St. Paul, an American express mail liner of 11,630 tons. Grounded on Sconce Point, the Gladiator rolled on to her starboard side. A blizzard was blowing and the St. Paul took 20 minutes to launch her lifeboats because the ropes and pulleys were choked with ice. Sailors dressed in heavy seaboots and oilskins were at the mercy of one of the most dangerous offshore tidal currents around Britain. The prompt action of the soldiers, one of whom waded in to save seven men before he himself had to be carried from the sea suffering from exposure and exhaustion, kept the death toll down to 29. It so happened that ten years to the day, on 25th April, 1918, the St. Paul mysteriously sank in New York Harbour. The fort was used for training purposes in World War II and abandoned in 1962. It now houses an aquarium and a museum.

Refreshments   There is a seasonal cafeteria at Fort Victoria.

Route 2

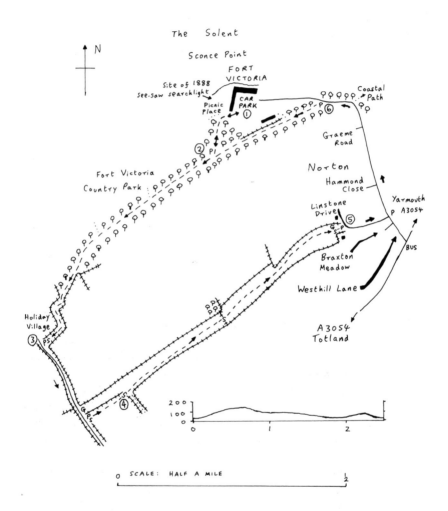

The Solent

Sconce Point

FORT VICTORIA

Site of 1888
See-saw searchlight

Picnic Place

CAR PARK ①

Coastal Path

⑥

Graeme Road

② Pl

Norton

Fort Victoria Country Park

Hammond Close

Linstone Drive

⑤

Yarmouth P A3054

BUS

Braxton Meadow

Westhill Lane

Holiday Village

③ PS

A3054 Totland

④

```
200
100
  0
     0        1        2
```

0   SCALE: HALF A MILE   ½

Route 2

Fort Victoria   2½ miles

START *Fort Victoria at the end of an access lane from the A3054 one mile west of Yarmouth. There is a car park at the fort. The nearest bus stop is for the No. 7 and 7A services between Ryde and Freshwater Bay via Newport and Yarmouth and is at Norton where the access lane leaves the A3054 (G.R. 339898 for Fort Victoria).*

ROUTE

1. *With the fort on your right go ahead towards the picnic place. Turn left along the path into the woodland. Pass numbered waymarked posts relating to a nature trail (No. 1 on your left, then No. 2 on your right). Climb up to a T-junction with the level Coastal Path, where a signpost points back towards Fort Victoria and its cafeteria.* 2. *Go right along the Coastal Path. Continue past a seat at a viewpoint on your right and through a coppiced section of the wood. Ascend a flight of steps ahead to gain a fine view across the Solent to the mainland, on your right. Continue out of the Country Park to follow a fenced path around a corner to your left, then to your right, with a holiday village behind the fence on your right.*

3. *Cross the stile beside a signpost ahead to join a lane (Monks Lane). Turn left along this, away from the holiday village. Look out for a stile beside a signpost for path F3 in about 350 metres on your left. Turn left across the stile to follow signposted path F3. Walk beside a fence on your left to a stile in the corner ahead.*

4. *Continue over the stile to walk up a long, narrow, field. Keep near the fence on your right before veering left to take a stile in a fence ahead. Maintain your direction up another long, narrow, field to reach a stile beside a gate in the far left corner ahead. Go ahead over it to reach a road, Linstone Drive, at a signpost.*

5. *Go right along Linstone Drive to a T-junction, where a public footpath signpost across the road points back towards where you have come from. THIS IS THE NEAREST POINT FOR PEOPLE REACHING THIS WALK BY BUS TO JOIN THE CIRCUIT FROM THE BUS STOP. Go left along the road, passing Hammond Close and Graeme Road on your left, then follow the road ahead as it bends left.*

6. *Take the signposted Coastal Path on your left, and turn right at the signpost for Fort Victoria and its cafeteria to return to the start.*

Public Transport Buses Nos. 7 or 7A (Ryde-Yarmouth-Freshwater Bay).

HEADING FOR ST. SWITHIN'S

16

Route 3   3 miles
St. Swithin's Church

Outline Yarmouth Castle ~ Old Mill ~ Mill Copse ~ St. Swithin's
Church ~ Coastal Path ~ Yarmouth Castle.

Summary An interesting old town stands beside the mouth of the River
Yar. This route goes beside the river to an old mill before cutting across a
dismantled railway line to visit the ruined St. Swithin's Church at
Thorley. A coastal promenade completes the circuit to Yarmouth.

Attractions Yarmouth basks in the glory of being mentioned in the
Domesday Book of 1086 and having its first Charter as a town granted in
1135, but the Domesday Book also reveals that nearby Thorley (then
valued at £12) was the port of this area (Yarmouth was valued at only 25
shillings). Thorley Creek soon silted up, leading to the growth of
Yarmouth as a port. It was deemed worth attacking by the French in 1377
and in 1524. Henry VIII invested in a castle here in 1547. This includes the
earliest English example of an arrow-head bastion. It was to remain
garrisoned until 1885. Tucked away from the street and overlooking the
sea, its low profile makes it easy to miss. It's well worth a visit, however.
The castle is in excellent repair and it is possible to compare the kitchen in
the Master Gunner's House with its modern counterpart.

The old tidal mill ground corn. Some of this came from the mainland,
making access by boat essential. Opened in 1793, it was recently owned
by the late A. J. P. Taylor, the historian. Oyster beds used to be a feature
of the River Yar near here. The birdlife of the estuary is still rich, with
cormorant, grey heron, shelduck, mallard, reed bunting, redshank,
lapwing, mute swan, coot and moorhen likely to be spotted. The railway
must have provided a scenic journey here on its route between Newport
and Freshwater. The first train to Yarmouth ran in 1888 and carried
V.I.P.'s standing in open cattle trucks. Despite this, the official opening
of the line in 1889 led the local journalist to wax lyrical on the health
benefits to be derived from rail travel. The 'gentle oscillatory motion of
the railway carriage' would improve the system 'by equalising circulation,
promoting digestion, tranquillising the nervous system, and, last but not
least, by inducing sleep on the succeeding night'. Insomnia returned to
Yarmouth when the line was closed in 1953!

The ruins of St. Swithin's Church at Thorley go back to the 13th
century, but the story of this saint is at least 400 years older.

Swithin's former pupil Ethelwulf, King of Wessex, chose him as
Bishop of Winchester in 852. Famous for his humility, charity and church-
continued on page 20

17

Route 3

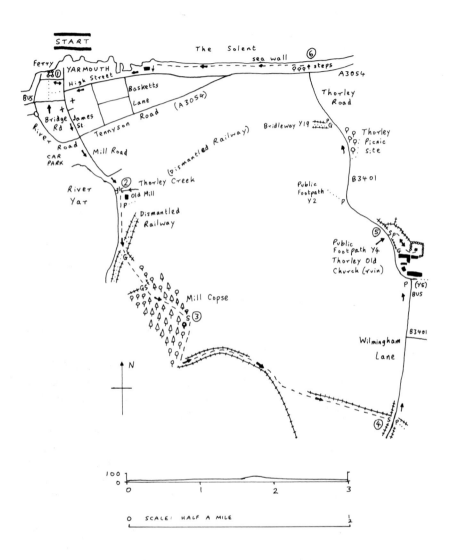

Route 3

St. Swithin's Church   3 miles

START   *Quay Street, Yarmouth, contains the local Tourist Information Centre, opposite which is the castle. As the ferry terminal and the bus station are nearby, this makes an excellent place to start. There is a car park inland of River Road (the A3054). Yarmouth Castle is in the care of English Heritage and is open from April to September between 10 a.m. and 6 p.m. (G.R. 354898).*

ROUTE

1. *Face Yarmouth Castle and go right to the Square. Turn right along James Street and across the busy A3054 to Mill Road. Continue up this road until it bends left. Go ahead along a path which has the River Yar on your right.*

2. *Cross a bridge over a stream and pass a tidal mill on your left. Pass the signposted path Y2 on your left and reach the line of a dismantled railway (now a bridleway). Cross it to take the gate ahead. Cross a field to woodland, which is entered by a stile beside a gate. Follow a path through the wood.*

3. *Leave the wood by an isolated stile (that has lost its fence). Turn right to the corner, and turn left along a hedged path. Emerge to walk with a hedge on your right for a further 250 metres, then bear left across the field to join a hedge and walk with it on your left.*

4. *Cross a stile in the corner to reach a road, and turn left along it. Join the B3401, which comes from your right, follow it round a bend to your left opposite a substantial farm on your right and look out for a stile beside a signpost for public footpath Y4 on your right.*

5. *Turn right across the signposted stile to follow path Y4 to the ruins of St. Swithin's Church, Thorley. Retrace your steps to the road and resume your previous direction. Pass a picnic site on your right and the line of the dismantled railway (now bridleway Y19) on your left. Go ahead across the A3054 with care and take steps to reach the Coastal Path on the sea wall.*

6. *Turn left along the Coastal Path to walk with the Solent on your right towards Yarmouth. When buildings block your way ahead, turn left to the road and go right to follow the pavement back into the centre of Yarmouth.*

Public Transport Wightlink run the ferry from Yarmouth to Lymington. Buses 7 and 7A serve Yarmouth from Ryde (via Newport) and Freshwater Bay.

19

building, Swithin died in 862. He asked to be buried in the cemetery outside the Old Minster. In 971, however, on 15th July, his remains were transferred inside the cathedral. A healer in his lifetime, many miraculous cures were attributed to his relics. Most of all, Swithin had a reputation for influencing the weather and if it rains on St. Swithin's Day (15th July) it will also rain for the following forty days. Now, druids could control the weather and they preferred to worship in the open air. Swithin was, no doubt, a Christian druid. His name is derived from sywedydd, the Welsh for magician (shaman, druid). Swithin was the mentor of Asser, the Welsh monk who became Alfred the Great's adviser.

Refreshments   There is a choice of shops in Yarmouth.

LOOKING BACK AT CARISBROOKE

20

Carisbrooke Castle

Outline St. Mary's Church, Carisbrooke ~ Priory Mill Pond ~ Carisbrooke Castle ~ Castle Lane ~ St. Mary's Church, Carisbrooke.

Summary This short ramble around the impressive Carisbrooke Castle includes a couple of fairly steep ascending paths. Why not take a break in the castle, where refreshments are available from a cafeteria?

Attractions The old pond of Priory Mill is now a pleasant lake fringed with willows and furnished with benches and picnic tables. If you're lucky, you might see a kingfisher. Also here are mallard, tufted duck, pochard, mandarin, muscovy duck, mute swan, Canada goose, moorhen, coot, water rail, pied wagtail, grey wagtail and little grebe. Jays and magpies inhabit the beech trees which shade the sunken path leading towards the castle.

Carisbrooke Castle is the only medieval castle on the Island and is the most impressive of all its ancient monuments. In the care of English Heritage, it is open daily all year except for Christmas Eve, Christmas Day, Boxing Day and New Year's Day, between 10 a.m. and 6 p.m. (4 p.m. from October to March). The views from it are superb, covering much of central Wight. This was probably an ancient site, used by Britons and Romans, but the earliest uncovered evidence is for a Saxon fort. This was needed as a defence against Viking raiders. The Normans admired its strategic position and Richard de Redvers constructed the motte-and-bailey (mound and courtyard) soon after it came into his possession in 1100. By 1136, stone walls had been added to both. The last of the family to hold the castle was the formidable widow and countess Isabella de Fortibus. She rebuilt and added to the castle before selling it to King Edward I on her deathbed in 1293. Her work was put to the test when the French invaded during the Hundred Years War in 1377. When the French leader was killed by an arrow shot by Peter Heynoe from an arrow slit still pointed out on the west side of the castle, the besiegers went back across the Channel demoralised.

The castle's most historic moment was when it became the prison for King Charles I prior to his execution in London on 30th January, 1649. Attempts were made, and bungled, to effect the king's escape. It is even possible that Oliver Cromwell would have welcomed a successful attempt to enable him to avoid having to execute the king. Afterwards, the unfortunate royal children were kept here and sad little Princess Elizabeth died in her bed on 8th September, 1650 after contracting

continued on page 24

21

Route 4

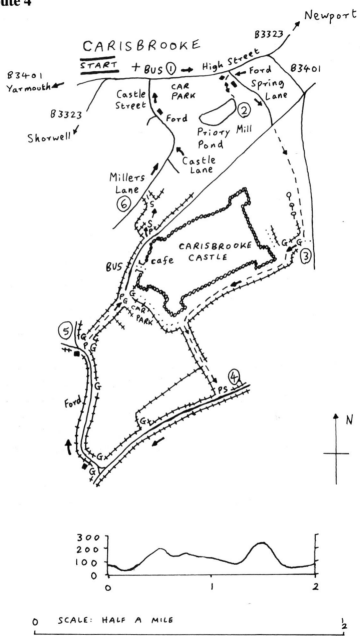

Route 4

Carisbrooke Castle   2 miles

START *The walk begins from the bus stop near the church in Carisbrooke High Street. There is a car park nearby (G.R. 486882).*

ROUTE

1. *With your back to St. Mary's Church, go left down Carisbrooke High Street, cross the road by the pelican crossing and continue until you reach a ford and Spring Lane on your right. Before going up this lane, take a path on your right which crosses a footbridge to reach a lake. This is the Priory Mill pond.*

2. *Retrace your steps to Spring Lane and turn right along it. Go ahead across a road at a T-junction and maintain your direction along a sunken path beneath beech trees.*

3. *Turn right through a gate to emerge on the grassy top of the dry moat around Carisbrooke Castle. Go left along this, with the castle across the moat on your right. Just before the corner, descend on your left to take a narrow, hedged, path away from the castle. Climb the opposite side of the valley with a fence on your right only.*

4. *Cross a stile beside a signpost to reach a lane. Go right along it. Take the first turning on your right down to a ford and continue to a lane junction.*

5. *Turn right up the enclosed path signposted as public footpath N88 to Carisbrooke Castle. This climbs steeply to emerge at the castle car park. Bear left along the access road to pass the castle entrance on your right. Go ahead past traffic lights, then bear left down steps. Continue down a field to a stile which leads to a short path giving access to Millers Lane.*

6. *Go right along the lane and follow it back to the High Street opposite St. Mary's Church.*

Public Transport Buses Nos. 1B, 1C, 7 and 7A (all between Ryde, Newport and Freshwater Bay by varying routes) all stop in Carisbrooke.

pneumonia after playing bowls in the rain. She wouldn't have seen the friends of all little children - the donkeys who tread a wheel to raise water from the well. They didn't replace human prisoners until the 18th century.

Refreshments   There is a cafeteria in Carisbrooke Castle.

STEAM TRAIN AT HAVENSTREET

24

Route 5 3½ miles
Havenstreet

Outline Havenstreet Station ~ White Hart Inn ~ Firestone Copse ~ Newnham Farm ~ War Memorial ~ St. Peter's Church, Havenstreet ~ Havenstreet Station.

Summary There seems to be a lot of road walking on this route, but most of it is along quiet lanes. They connect splendid paths through a forest and across fields to a viewpoint. This is one walk which you must come to by train - and steam train at that!

Attractions The infamous Beeching Report of 1963 led to the closure of British Rail's line between Smallbrook Junction (for Ryde) and Cowes via Newport on 21st February, 1966. The line between Cowes and Newport had been the Island's first railway, opening on 16th June, 1862. The section through Havenstreet linking Newport with the surviving Ryde to Shanklin line opened on 20th December, 1875. By 1971 enthusiastic volunteers had established the Isle of Wight Steam Railway at Havenstreet. The locomotive 'Calbourne' and six carriages had been acquired when British Rail ended steam on their remaining Island Line. A mere one and a half miles of track was saved between Havenstreet and Wootton, where a new station had to be opened in 1986. Further progress to Newport is proving difficult but this brave little railway is no longer isolated. The three and a half miles of track to Smallbrook Junction have been relaid, and it is possible to step off a British Rail electric train there to connect with one of the growing band of steam trains now maintained at Havenstreet. Steam trains run on a seasonal basis, so plan ahead for this trip and telephone 0983 882204 or send an s.a.e. to the Station Manager, The Railway Station, Havenstreet, Isle of Wight, PO33 4DS, for a current timetable. The station at Havenstreet has a souvenir shop and refreshment room, plus a museum and an adventure playground.

Firestone Copse is one of several Forestry Commission woodlands on the Island which have waymarked walks and picnic places. Leaflets describing these should be available from local Tourist Information Centres - the others are Brighstone Forest and Parkhurst Forest. The 247 acres include plantations of conifers, such as Corsican pine, Douglas fir and Lawson cypress, but the native oak trees are also here. The trees give shelter to winter walks, when the purple shoots of dogwood can be seen. Wild daffodils and primrose brighten the Spring (but they are not to be picked!). Butterflies abound in summer. Look out for white and red admirals, marbled whites, small tortoiseshells, gatekeepers and

continued on page 28

25

Route 5

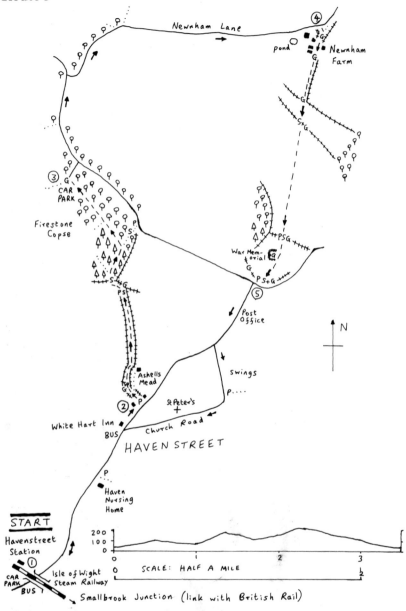

Newnham Lane

pond

Newnham Farm

CAR PARK

Firestone Copse

PSG

War Memorial

Post Office

swings

Ashells Mead

St Peter's

White Hart Inn

BUS

Church Road

HAVEN STREET

Haven Nursing Home

START

Havenstreet Station

CAR PARK

BUS

Isle of Wight Steam Railway

Smallbrook Junction (link with British Rail)

N

SCALE: HALF A MILE

Route 5

Havenstreet

3½ miles

START *Havenstreet Railway Station is south of the village on the minor road between Newport and Ryde (G.R. 556898).*

ROUTE

1. *From the station, go left along the road into Havenstreet. Ignore a signposted path on your right just after Haven Nursing Home. Fork left (i.e. go ahead) at the White Hart Inn and pass the village telephone box on your left.*

2. *Turn left down the signposted public footpath R6 to Firestone. Don't take the private access to Ashells Mead on your right, but do bear right just after it to cross a stile and follow the enclosed path. Emerge over another stile and go left to find a third stile on your right. This leads into Firestone Copse. Bear right along a path between the trees for about 100 metres before turning left along a path dividing the conifers on your left from broadleaved trees on your right. Pass a red waymarked post and go ahead to the car park. If you have time and the Forestry Commission leaflet, you could extend this route by diverting around one of the waymarked trails.*

3. *Go right to leave the forest by its access drive. Turn left along a road and go right when you come to a junction. This is Newnham Lane and is signposted for Binstead. Follow this lane until you pass the pond and buildings of Newnham Farm on your right.*

4. *Turn right immediately after the farm to leave the lane as it bears left. Take a gate to walk through the farmyard to another gate. Go ahead beside a fence on your left. Continue through a third gate and across a field to a stile to the right of a gate ahead. Maintain your direction to a stile beside a signpost and a gate in the fence ahead, climbing to meet trees on your right. Go ahead to pass the war memorial at the 200 ft. summit and descend to the road ahead.*

5. *Go straight ahead along the road which passes the village Post Office on your left. Fork left to pass swings on your left, then bend right with Church Road to pass St. Peter's Church on your right. Return to face the White Hart Inn and go left down the road to retrace your steps to Havenstreet Railway Station.*

Public Transport Rejoice in the fact that you can still come here by train and do so via Smallbrook Junction (on British Rail's line between Ryde and Shanklin). Telephone 0983 882204 for train times. There is also the No. 7 or 7A bus (between Ryde and Freshwater Bay via Newport).

fritillaries. The red berries of the guelder rose make autumn a special season. The highpoint of this walk is only at 200 feet, but a panoramic view can be had. Here is Havenstreet's unusual war memorial.

Refreshments   Havenstreet Railway Station.

NODES BEACON

28

Route 6   3 miles
Alum Bay

Outline   The Needles Pleasure Park, Alum Bay ~ Nodes Beacon ~ West High Down ~ The Needles Batteries ~ The Needles Pleasure Park.

Summary   This is one of the best walks in the whole of England, let alone the Isle of Wight. West High Down is full of fairy rings, which may explain the enchantment. The walk above the cliffs is spectacular, while the return route faces the multi-coloured cliffs of Alum Bay. The diversion into the Needles Batteries is worth the admission fee for the close-up view of the Needles alone. Finish with a ride on the chair lift down to those famous sands.

Attractions   Don't stray into the Needles Pleasure Park at the start, or you could miss a memorable walk. Keep its treat for the end, when you can take the chair lift to the beach and scoop your own various shades of sand. Ornamental glassware can be bought to display the sand and a relaxing time can be had watching this being made in Alum Bay Glass. This is open daily from Easter to October, 10 a.m.-5 p.m. It is also open during the winter from Mondays to Fridays, 10 a.m.-1 p.m. and 2-5 p.m. No glass is made on Saturdays. There are over 20 different shades of the sand, which show up best on the cliffs after rain. Boat trips to view the Needles are available on the beach.

The Needles are composed of chalk, which has suffered considerably from erosion over the years. The name of these rocks actually refers to a tall 'needle' of chalk, 120 feet high, which toppled into the sea in 1764. These rocks have also had their share of shipwrecks, including the biggest sailing ship to be totally wrecked on the island's coastline. This was the 2347 ton 'Irex' and the rescue of 29 out of the 36 aboard her on 25th January, 1890, is a tale of extraordinary bravery against overwhelming odds. Her voyage had started on 10th December, 1889, from Greenock, bound for Rio de Janeiro with a cargo of iron, pipes and pots. Tremendous gales forced her back to Greenock, then to Belfast and, finally well off-course, to here. The captain had been driven beyond the point of exhaustion and was hallucinating when he imagined the Needles Light to be a pilot boat. The lifeboat was forced back before reaching the wreck and the rescue was effected by a rocket trailing a rope fired from the fort. The rope caught on a rock and Coastguard Mayo climbed down to free it.

The batteries fortifying the cliffs above the Needles were erected when a French invasion was feared in the time of Napoleon III. They

continued on page 32

29

Route 6

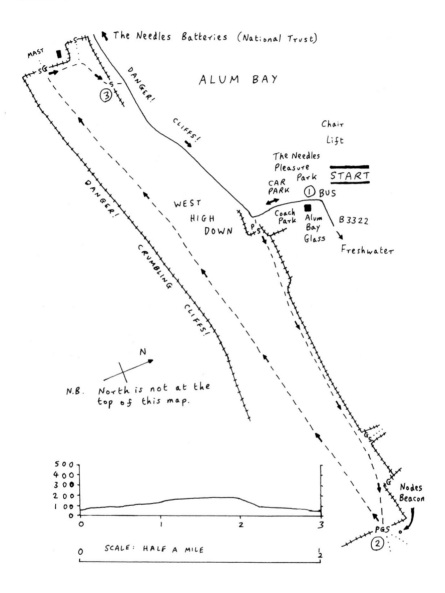

The Needles Batteries (National Trust)

ALUM BAY

MAST
SG
③
DANGER!
CLIFFS!

Chair
Lift

The Needles
Pleasure
Park
CAR
PARK
① BUS
START

WEST
HIGH
DOWN

DANGER!

CRUMBLING

CLIFFS!

Coach
Park
Alum
Bay
Glass

P.S.

B 3322

Freshwater

N

N.B. North is not at the
top of this map.

500
400
300
200
100
0

0   1   2   3

SCALE: HALF A MILE

0   ½

G.S.

G
Nodes
Beacon

PGS
②

30

Route 6

Alum Bay   3 miles

START   *The Needles Pleasure Park above Alum Bay has a large car park and is the terminus for the 1B and 1C bus services from Ryde via Newport. You can also take the chair lift up from the beach (G.R. 308855).*

ROUTE

1. *With your back to the sea and facing Alum Bay Glass, go right up the road until it bends right. Turn left here to a stile. Cross it to follow the signposted public footpath T25 towards Tennyson Down. Go ahead with a fence on your left. Pass a gate beside a stile on your left, opposite an old chalk pit on your right. Ignore a gate in the corner which juts out ahead. Veer right to the stile beside a gate and a signpost in the fence beyond it, near the half-size replica of the Old Nodes Beacon.*

2. *Turn sharply right without having crossed the stile. Follow the signposted Coastal Path, here T24. A glorious walk along West High Down with the crumbling cliffs and the sea on your left feels like paradise on a sunny day. Eventually you reach a stile beside a gate and before a mast ahead. Turn right before it to descend, and bear right down to a stile in the bottom fence.*

3. *Cross the stile to reach the access road to the Needles Batteries, which are well worth a short diversion to the left. Go right along the road to follow it back to the start of this walk.*

Public Transport   Buses Nos. 1B and 1C from Ryde via Newport.

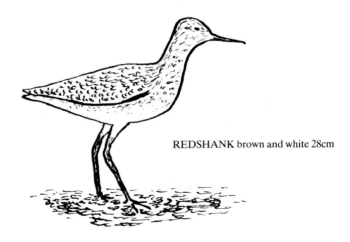

REDSHANK brown and white 28cm

didn't see action until Hitler had a go nearly one hundred years later. The first British anti-aircraft gun was mounted here in 1913, while the Black Knight space rocket was tested here in the 1950s.

Refreshments   The Needles Pleasure Park.

THE TENNYSON MEMORIAL

Tennyson Down

Outline Totland Bay Youth Hostel ~ Farringford ~ Tennyson Down ~ Totland Bay Youth Hostel.

Summary A moderate walk along lanes, fieldpaths and hedged bridleways has a steep climax which is aided by the provision of steps along the path to the Tennyson Memorial.

Attractions Don't think that youth hostels are not for you! If you're using this book, they are probably the very places for you to base the family whilst enjoying the countryside. You'll also meet lots of interesting people, both hostellers and wardens. Nowadays the emphasis is more on the buildings and facilities, which does attract certain types who wouldn't dream of entering a youth hostel without their modern conveniences. The spirit is still the thing, however. Y.H.A. used to be popularly known as standing for 'Your Husband Assured'. Presumably, families are no longer in that market. The Y.H.A. is definitely in the market for them, however, with family annexes and family rooms on offer at a growing number of hostels. Many more offer small rooms with a few bunk beds for the exclusive use of families. This is vital if you are, for example, a father hostelling with daughters and they are too young (under 14) to sleep in a separate dormitory from their parent. Family Bunk Rooms can also let under-fives come hostelling (at the warden's discretion). If you can arrange for children and parents of the same sex to hostel together, and the children are over 5, you can always share the usual dormitories with other hostellers. This can be great fun. I well remember taking my son David on a hostelling trek up the Wye Valley. A party of youths walking the Offa's Dyke Path had the same itinerary and we all met up again each evening like Chaucer's Pilgrims.

One parent hostelling with one child is probably better than the whole family going as there is a better chance of mixing with other hostellers. Board games are usually available in hostel common rooms and somebody can usually be found to play with. If you have a child who is under 5 and want to stay together but find there isn't any family accommodation available (it's best to book it in advance), you could always camp in the grounds of the hostel (check the current Y.H.A. handbook to see which hostels have space for camping). Introducing children to both walking and youth hostelling should give them a good start to life. Full details are available from the Youth Hostels Association, Trevelyan House, 8 St. Stephen's Hill, St. Alban's, Hertfordshire, AL1 2DY. *continued on page 36*

continued on page 36

Route 7

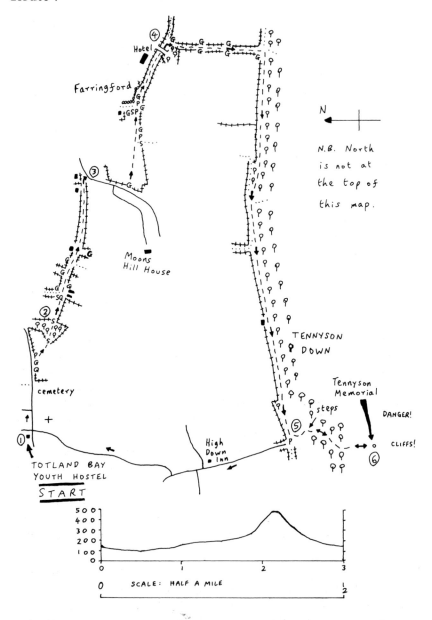

N

N.B. North is not at the top of this map.

④ Hotel

Farringford

③

Moons Hill House

②

cemetery

① TOTLAND BAY YOUTH HOSTEL

START

Moons Hill House

TENNYSON DOWN

Tennyson Memorial

DANGER!

⑤ steps

High Down Inn

⑥ CLIFFS!

500
400
300
200
100
0

0   1   2   3

0   SCALE: HALF A MILE   ½

34

Route 7

Tennyson Down

3 miles

START *This is a walk for families staying at Totland Bay youth hostel, where a family bunk room may be available and camping is possible in the grounds. If you're not staying here, it's not far to walk from the bus stop at Totland war memorial, from which you go left up Weston Road and take the second left at the top of a short hill, opposite a church. The nearby cul-de-sac (Cranstoun Close) may offer a parking space for a considerate motorist (G.R. 324865 - N.B. ignore former youth hostel at G.R. 345862 on old maps).*

ROUTE

1. *Face the church and go left along Summers Lane. You soon pass Cranstoun Close, St. Saviours Road and the signposted path T10 on your left. Bear right through a small gate beside a fieldgate and a signpost to cross a field to a copse. Cross a stile to follow the path between the trees.*

2. *Emerge over a second stile and go ahead with a fence on your right. Continue over a stile beside a gate and go ahead along a rough lane to join a road.*

3. *Go right along the road. Pass the drive to Moons Hill House, then turn left through a kissing-gate. Go ahead across a field, converging with a hedge on your right. Ignore a signposted stile for path F43 in it but take bridleway F47 ahead. Pass under the small wooden bridge. (Alfred Lord Tennyson had built so that he could walk from his garden, on your left, through the copse on your right, and up to the High Down without people noticing him leaving the house).*

4. *Turn right along the bridleway that Tennyson used. Follow it to the foot of the Down now named after the poet. Turn right to walk with the trees on your left for about one mile.*

5. *When a road comes up from your right, turn left along an uphill path which has been made easier by the creation of steps. Go through the trees to emerge on the bare grass of Tennyson Down. Go ahead to the celtic cross that serves as a memorial for Tennyson.*

6. *Retrace your steps down through the trees and go ahead along the road. Ignore turnings and follow it back to the youth hostel.*

Public Transport Buses Nos. 1B and 1C from Ryde via Newport and Freshwater Bay and Nos. 7 and 7A from Ryde via Newport and Yarmouth.

Tennyson is the theme of this walk. The great Victorian poet loved to stride along these paths and to breathe the air on top of the cliffs. He reckoned it was worth 'sixpence a pint'. It inspired him to write 'The Charge of the Light Brigade' and 'The Idylls of the King' whilst living at nearby Farringford. It was Tennyson's home between 1853 and 1892 and is now a hotel. Amongst his visitors were Sir Arthur Sullivan, Charles Darwin, Lewis Carroll, Charles Kingsley, Henry Longfellow, Garibaldi and Albert the Prince Consort. Tennyson composed special poems to serve as written invitations to his guests. After an impoverished start to life, Tennyson became wealthy and famous, succeeding William Wordsworth as poet laureate. Benjamin Jowett, from the famous Oxford scholastic family, was one of his regular visitors, as was Sir James Knowles, editor of the 'Contemporary Review'. Sir James became the architect of Tennyson's second home, built on the mainland, in Surrey, to avoid the crowds of summer tourists flocking to Farringford. Tennyson still lived on the Island in the winter after his Surrey home was built in 1868. It must have been a wrench for him to leave here, even seasonally, but his admirers used to climb trees to spy on him.

Most of the downland is now owned by the National Trust. As its highest point (482 feet) stands a Celtic cross, erected in 1897 as a memorial to Tennyson. The inscription reads 'In memory of Alfred Lord Tennyson. This was raised as a Beacon to Sailors by the people of Freshwater and other Friends in England and America'.

Refreshments In Totland (or at the hostel, if you are staying there).

FRESHWATER BAY

Afton Down

Outline   Freshwater Bay ~ Afton Down ~ Fort Redoubt ~ Freshwater Bay.

Summary   A fairly energetic climb up Afton Down is rewarded by splendid views. Watch out for golf balls on the way down! Be careful too when the clifftop path approaches Freshwater Bay, but you can safely go down steps to play on the beach. The Redoubt gives a fine view back over the rest of the walk.

Attractions   Bronze Age tumuli or round barrows (plus an off-route long barrow dating from the New Stone Age) demonstrate the prehistoric nature of these chalk tracks. These chalklands were extensively cleared of trees by the people who left the earthworks. It is the marks left by nature that will linger in the memory from this walk. The views from Afton Down can be astounding on a fine day, with the Yar Estuary, the Solent and the mainland laid at your feet. Dorset doesn't seem far away and the coastal scenery here is as impressive as Lulworth Cove. Freshwater Bay is a superb semi-circle set amidst tall white cliffs. Its magic attracted George Bernard Shaw, who started to write 'Caesar and Cleopatra' here. Notice the three prominent rocks named the Arch, Stag and Mermaid. The small fort or redoubt was built in 1855-56, when a French invasion was feared. The colonel's wife entertained Queen Victoria and four year old Princess Beatrice to tea here in 1860. You can now enjoy tea here too.

Refreshments   A choice of places in Freshwater Bay, including the Redoubt.

Route 8

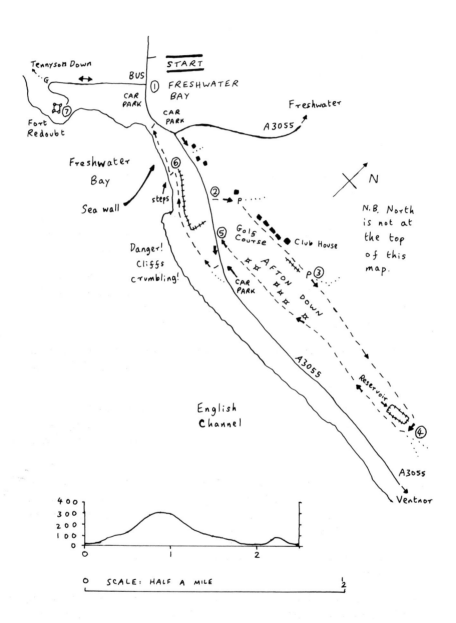

Route 8

Afton Down   2½ miles

START   *The bus stop at Freshwater Bay is near one of the car parks and the public toilets (G.R. 345858).*

ROUTE

1. *With your back to the lane to Fort Redoubt (signposted as path F50 Tennyson Trail) and with the public toilets on your left, go right along the road towards the sea at Freshwater Bay. Go right at the fork to follow the A3055 (Military Road) towards Ventnor, with the English Channel on your right.*

2. *Bear left up a track named Southdown Road. Reach a signpost and bear right along bridleway F54 (Freshwater Way). Follow the access track to the Club House of the golf course and continue to another signpost.*

3. *Ignore bridleway F32 (Freshwater Way) descending on your left. Keep climbing gradually along the chalk track ahead. Near the top of Afton Down, where the views all around are memorable, make a U turn, keeping the fence of a reservoir on your right.*

4. *Descend gradually back towards Freshwater Bay, which is ahead with Tennyson Down above and beyond it. This grassy track is bridleway F33. Pass several tumuli on the golf course.*

5. *Reach the A3055 near another car park and go left along it for about 100 yards, then cross the road carefully to join a clear path. Turn right along this towards Freshwater Bay and walk with the sea on your left. Keep away from dangerous cliff edges.*

6. *Take steps on your left down to the sea wall and follow this around the bay to the Albion Hotel. Go right to join the road, and turn left along it back to the start of this walk. Continue, however, by taking the access lane to Fort Redoubt on your left.*

7. *Retrace your steps to the public toilets, bus stop and car park at the start of this walk.*

Public Transport   Freshwater Bay is served by buses Nos. 1B and 1C from Ryde via Newport and Nos. 7 and 7A from Ryde via Newport and Yarmouth.

BERNARD SHAW. WAX MUSEUM, BRADING

Calbourne Mill

Outline   Calbourne Mill ~ Calbourne ~ Westover Downs ~ Calbourne Mill.

Summary   This walk shows the charm of the Island's interior, with an old mill, downland tracks, patches of woodland and well-maintained fieldpaths.

Attractions   Calbourne is an unspoilt village, complete with its old pump. St. Mary's Church is built on land granted by King Egbert in 826. Westover House isn't open to the public, but you can see the ducks on its lake. The Caul Bourne (the stream) used to power five mills on its way north from the village that is named after it. One is now open to the public, while its millpond and stretch of the stream have been turned into attractive gardens. The earliest reference to this mill appears to be in the Domesday Book of 1086. It seems there were two mills under one roof, one for wheat and one for malt and the name was Mylplace. The complex included a house and a malthouse. By 1697 it was worth £60 in a sale. A record of the owners over the last 400 years has been kept. One interesting character is a J. A. Long who evidently left being a schoolmaster at Pembroke Dock to be the miller of Calbourne from 1869 to 1878. He sold it to the Weeks family, led by George Weeks, an accountant of Brixton Rise, London. It is still in their hands.

Watching the water wheel turn is an absorbing pastime. It can come as a surprise to realise that over 1000 tons of water can flow over it in an hour. This is over 250,000 gallons, from 48 buckets being filled at a rate of about six times a minute and containing up to 13½ gallons of water (about 135 lbs.) each time. Inside, the first floor of the mill is occupied by grinding stones. Other old implements are on display. The granary is on the top floor. The roof timbers are reputedly from a shipwreck at Brook. Brook Bay is famous for its dinosaur remains and some interesting fossils have been brought to the mill for display. A regular supply of water is vital - hence the sluice gates in the millpond. Calbourne Mill survived because it introduced the roller plant, replacing its grinding stones, in the late 19th century. This produced finer, whiter, flour. This flour was also stable and could be sold to bakers. As a result, the mill's own bakehouse and bread delivery rounds closed down. A steam engine operated the roller plant until 1920 when a suction gas engine replaced it until the roller plant stopped being used in 1955. Since then, the mill has been a tourist attraction and a museum of rural life. Included in the exhibits are washing

continued on page 44

41

Route 9

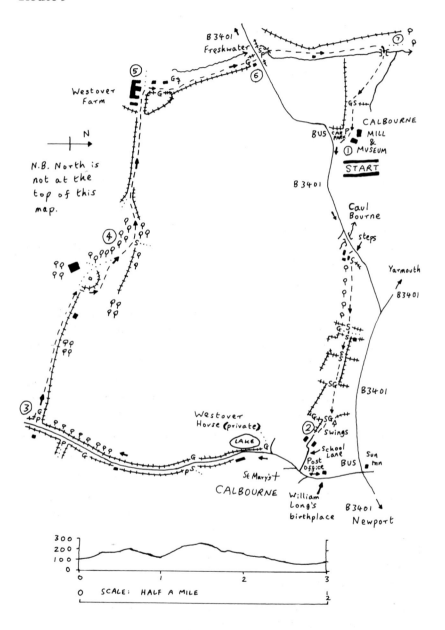

B 3401
Freskwater

⑤ Westover Farm

⑦

⑥

GS

CALBOURNE
MILL
&
MUSEUM

BUS CAR PARK

①

START

B 3401

N.B. North is not at the top of this map.

→ N

Caul Bourne

steps

④

Yarmouth

B3401

③

B 3401

Westover House (private)

LAKE

② Swings

School Lane

Post Office

St Mary's

CALBOURNE

William Long's birthplace

Sun Inn

BUS

B 3401
Newport

300
200
100
0

0   1   2   3

0   SCALE: HALF A MILE   ½

Route 9

Calbourne Mill

3 miles

START *Buses stop at the entrance to the Water Mill and Museum of Rural Life at Calbourne, where there is also a car park (G.R. 415868).*

ROUTE

1. *With your back to the Mill, go left, carefully, along the B3401 towards the village of Calbourne. Shortly after crossing a bridge over a stream (Caul Bourne), pass a farm on your right and immediately turn right up a flight of steps to a stile. Cross it and follow the path along the right hand side of the field (which may have maize growing in it) to another stile. Go ahead over this, a track and a third stile. Maintain this direction across three more fields with stiles inbetween them. Finally, pass swings on your left as you reach the village of Calbourne.*

2. *Go down School Lane to reach the road that runs through Calbourne, passing the Post Office on your left. Divert left up the road to see the plaque on a house on your left, which commemorates the fact that William Long, author of the Isle of Wight Dialect Dictionary and editor of the Oglander Memoirs was born here on 6th October, 1839. Turn round to follow the road past the old village pump and St. Mary's Church on your left, then a lake near the entrance to Westover House on your right. Continue until a bridleway is signposted on your right.*

3. *Turn right up the signposted bridleway CB16B to Westover Downs. Follow this track until a gap in the fence on your right is waymarked with an arrow. Go right, then bear left back to the track.*

4. *Follow the track past woodland on your left, ignore a waymarked stile on your right and continue to the farmyard of Westover Farm.*

5. *Turn right in the farmyard to follow a track back to the B3401 road.*

6. *Cross the road carefully and take the signposted stile slightly to the left of where you were. Cross the little footbridge immediately after it and go ahead near the stream on your right.*

7. *Shortly before the trees ahead, turn right over a bridge across the stream and walk to a stile beside a gate in the far right corner of the field. Continue over it to reach the Mill.*

Public Transport The No. 1C bus between Ryde, Newport, Freshwater and Alum Bay stops outside both Calbourne Mill and the Sun Inn, Calbourne.

machines. This is a good place for a picnic (refreshments are available), but mind that the peacocks don't peck the food from your lips!

Refreshments Calbourne Mill provides teas, while there is a shop near the Sun Inn, Calbourne.

CARAVAN AT ARRETON

Route 10

Arreton Manor

Outline   Robin Hill Country Park ~ Gallows Hill ~ Shepherd's Lane ~ Arreton Manor ~ Robin Hill Country Park.

Summary   The beautiful downland in the heart of the Island is covered by ancient tracks which give inspiring views and lead to interesting places.

Attractions   Robin Hill Country Park, at the start of this walk, should be left until the end, or you may spend all day in its 80 acres. Open daily between March and October from 10 a.m. to 5 p.m., the admission charge allows you to sample the delights of the Santa Fe railway, safari cars, B.M.X. bikes, a toboggan ride and a golf course which requires you to tee off from an island in the lake.

Gallows Hill is the place to be if you are at all psychic, especially at night around 'Old Christmas Eve' (4th January). A doctor was driving past here then in 1969 and reported a ghostly vision of what appeared to be an ancient battle. Bronze Age round barrows are sited here, while the name is significant. Gallows were often erected where leys crossed, so that the earth could dissipate the negative energies. Micah Moorey's body was hung here in 1776 and the gallows post now forms a beam in the nearby Hare and Hounds.

Allow plenty of time and bring money for admission fees because the splendid Arreton Manor is also on this route. The Elizabethan house incorporates parts of the 14th century farmhouse built by the monks of Quarr Abbey, while archaeological finds indicate that this is an ancient site. Built in a typical 'E' shape, its rooms are richly panelled and furnished. Eight monarchs have owned a house on this site, including Alfred the Great, who bequeathed it to his son Ethelward near the end of the ninth century. A copy of King Alfred's will can be seen in the Long Room, which also contains the original will of Barnaby Leigh, the tenant during the reign of Queen Elizabeth I. Sadly, Barnaby's son John murdered his sister here, but her ghost seems to be happy, playing around the house and garden. Perhaps little Annabel enjoys secret midnight sessions in the Museum of Childhood. This contains a wonderful range of toys and dolls, including the Pomeroy Regency Dolls House. The National Wireless Museum is also here. Arreton Manor is open from Easter to October, daily except on Saturdays.

Visitors can watch boats being built and jewellers at work in the Arreton Country Craft Village. Nearby stands St. George's Church, where a brass memorial can be found to Harry Hawles who fought at the

continued on page 48

45

Route 10

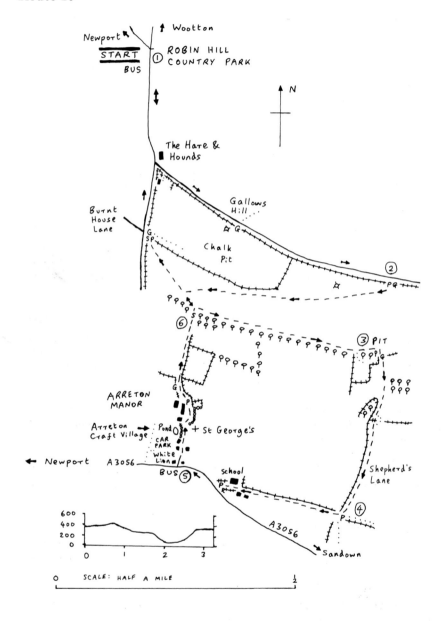

46

Route 10

Arreton Manor

3¼ miles

START *Robin Hill Country Park has a car park for those who pay the admission fee, while there are car parks for patrons at the Hare and Hounds and at Arreton Manor and Country Craft Village, where there is a bus stop for a different service. With so much adventure in store at Robin Hill, it's better to start and finish there (G.R. 533878).*

ROUTE

1. *With your back to the entrance to Robin Hill Country Park, go left to reach the Hare and Hounds. Fork left here for over half a mile along the crest of Gallows Hill.*

2. *Take a gate on your right, beside a signpost. Bear right along the footpath which descends very gradually to meet the perimeter fence of a chalk pit on your right. Continue descending to join another path and turn sharply left down it. Turn left to keep above the trees overlooking the vale on your right. Eventually, reach an old chalk pit.*

3. *Descend very carefully just before the chalk pit to emerge from the trees at its floor. Turn right through a gate and go ahead across a field, passing woodland on your left. Go ahead through a gap in the next hedge and continue along Shepherd's Lane (public footpath A13) with a hedge on your right to reach a signpost at a crosstracks.*

4. *Turn right along public bridleway A9, keeping the hedge on your right. Pass the school on your way to the road at Arreton and go right to reach the White Lion Hotel.*

5. *Just before the White Lion, turn right to reach St. George's Church. Continue past Arreton Manor on your left. Follow a fence on your right to climb gradually towards the trees ahead.*

6. *Go up steps to a stile, cross it and bear left. Climb to the far left corner of the down, where a signpost stands beside a stile. Go over this to the road and turn right along it to pass the Hare and Hounds on your right and reach Robin Hill Country Park.*

Public Transport Buses Nos. 3A (between Newport and Sandown) and 8 (between Ryde and Shanklin) serve Robin Hill, while No. 3 (between Cowes and Sandown via Newport) serves Arreton.

Battle of Agincourt in 1415. In the churchyard lie the bodies of Elizabeth Warbridge, the heroine of 'The Dairyman's Daughter' and her sister Hannah. They feature in Leigh Richmond's book 'The Annals of the Poor'.

Refreshments Available at Robin Hill Country Park and at Arreton Manor.

THE MAZE AT MORTON MANOR

Morton Manor

Outline Brading Station ~ Morton Manor ~ Roman Villa ~ Brading
Down ~ Nunwell Down ~ Wax Museum ~ Brading Station.

Summary Lanes, fieldpaths and downland tracks connect so many
places of interest that you'll have to ration the time spent at each one and
have plenty of money for admission fees. You could, of course, pass them
by and enjoy a picnic on the down and hide-and-seek in the wood.

Attractions Morton Manor is tucked away in a quiet corner, but it is a
real delight and well worth visiting. Beautiful gardens lead to a vineyard.
This was established in 1981 and the superb site and climate produce
excellent wine. As if the sight of dangling grapes isn't exotic enough,
there is a pagoda. Children are catered for with a fine play area near a turf
maze. The manor is open daily, except Saturdays, from the first Sunday in
April to the end of October, between 10 a.m. and 5.30 p.m.

You'll have to make your visit between April and September to see
the Roman Villa, which is open daily from 10 a.m. (10.30 a.m. on
Sundays) to 5.30 p.m. There are fine examples of mosaic floors dating
from the third century A.D. The villa's hypocaust (underfloor heating
system) can also be seen. This is arguably the best preserved Roman Villa
in Britain.

Back in Brading, don't miss the Lilliput Antique Doll and Toy
Museum. Little girls will love this, but little boys will find model trains
and cars and even a doll of Hitler. One doll has a handkerchief wrapped
as a bandage around its head. The little girl who owned it had been given
the doll on her birthday just before the Great War. Unfortunately, she
dropped it and broke its head. The doll has been made in Germany and a
new head couldn't be imported because of the war. Opening hours (daily)
are 10 a.m. to 5 p.m. in the winter and 9.30 a.m. to 9.30 p.m. in the
summer.

The Wax Museum is also open daily, even over Christmas (10 a.m. to
5 p.m. in the winter and 10 a.m. to 10 p.m. in the summer). Scenes and
characters from the Island's history are vividly recreated. This is the place
to see the Roman Vespasian in his chariot, Queen Victoria, King Charles
I, the little chimney sweep Valentine Grey, Little Jane of the Rev. Leigh
Richmond's book 'Annals of the Poor', the scandalous Sophie Dawes and
the scene in the Chapel of Rest when a young lady thought dead and
about to be buried opened the lid of her coffin. The real fun lies in the
Chamber of Horrors, where all sorts of executions, mutilations and

continued on page 52

Route 11

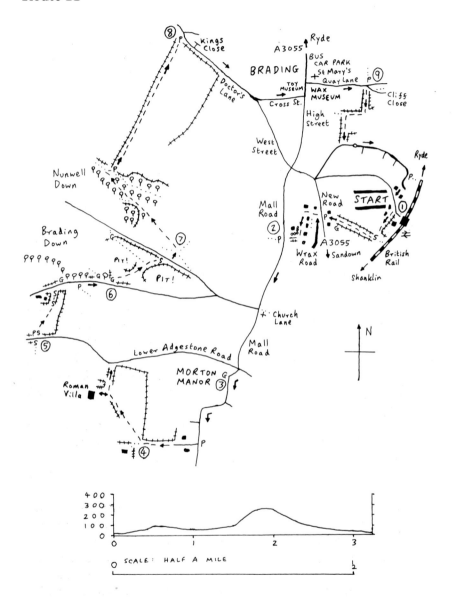

Route 11
Morton Manor
3¼ miles

START   *Brading has a station on the Island's surviving British Rail line, which makes it easy to reach on day-trips from Portsmouth via Ryde. Cars can be parked near the bus stop in Brading High Street or near the station (G.R. 610869).*

ROUTE

1. *Go ahead just a few metres along the station access road then turn left to walk with a fence on your left and houses on your right. Turn right along an enclosed path to New Road. Go ahead up the unmetalled Wrax Road opposite and follow it as it bends left. Turn right to reach Mall Road.*

2. *Turn left and follow Mall Road past Church Lane on your left, then Lower Adgestone Road on your right. Reach the gateway to Morton Manor on your right.*

3. *Continue past Morton Manor on your right. Turn right when you reach the signposted public footpath B48.*

4. *Bear right to the Roman Villa. Continue along the hedged path and go down steps to Lower Adgestone Road. Turn left along it.*

5. *After about ¼ mile turn right to cross a stile and follow the signposted public footpath B46. Go over a stile to take the fenced path to a road. Go right along it and pass the signposted path B65 on your right.*

6. *Bear left through a small gate beside a fieldgate to follow a path between two old chalk pits. Take a stile in the far right corner to reach a road, go right along it a few metres, then turn left along an obvious path to a path junction.*

7. *Bear left to continue through woodland and descend to a path running along the foot of the wood. Turn right to a signpost, and turn left to follow path B27 along the edge of the field on your right.*

8. *Reach a road and go right back towards Brading. Fork left to reach the High Street near the Toy Museum and the Wax Museum. Go left towards St. Mary's Church to see the stocks and whipping pole on your right. Go back a pace or two to Quay Lane and walk up it, passing the Wax Museum on your right and Ye Olde Pound on your left.*

9. *When a path is signposted on your left, turn right down a path opposite it. Reach a marshy waste and go right, then left, to emerge on a road. Go left along this and cut between buildings at its end to return to Brading station.*

Public Transport   British Rail trains from Ryde and Shanklin. Brading is also served by buses Nos. 16 and 16B between Ryde and Ventnor.

tortures can be witnessed. The same complex houses Animal World, with its stuffed creatures.

The Old Town Hall stands between the Wax Museum and St. Mary's Church. Here can be seen the old stocks and whipping post. These were in use well into the 19th century and were more economical than prison sentences. They also provided the public with a free form of entertainment. Stocks are fairly common around the country, but whipping posts are rare.

Refreshments   Morton Manor and a choice of places in Brading.

CLIFF EDGE, BROOK BAY

Brook Bay

Outline   Shippards Chine ~ Compton Grange ~ The Hamstead Trail ~ Badger Lane ~ Brook ~ Brook Chine ~ Hanover Point ~ Shippards Chine.

Summary   Pleasant inland tracks to Brook lead you to complete a circle by following the Coastal Path above Brook Bay. This is both spectacular and potentially dangerous - keep away from the crumbling cliff edges!

Attractions   The crumbling cliffs are composed of Wealden Marls and have revealed the fossilised bones of dinosaurs. Their story goes back some 120 million years, to the beginning of the Cretaceous period. Eurasia and North America then formed one huge mass of land called Laurasia. The Weald of Kent and Sussex was then a large lagoon connected to a northern sea. Low-lying land surrounded the lagoon and the Isle of Wight formed part of this land. A slow-flowing river crossed it from what is now the western end of the English Channel. The climate was subtropical and the area was a large swamp during the wet season. The red clays of the Wealden Marls were laid down in this. With them are found the dinosaur bones. Protected by burial under late deposits, the Wealden Marls have been exposed by comparatively recent folding. Rapid erosion is now providing a constant supply of fossils.

Many dinosaur bones end up on the beach and are destroyed by the sea. When they are found still in place in the cliff, they can be studied and identified. Vertebrae tend to survive the ravages of time better than skulls, which are hollow and fragile. As dinosaurs shed teeth and replaced them with new ones throughout their lives, teeth are fairly common and may not indicate the former presence of a skull.

Dinosaurs include the 'lizard-hipped' Saurischia and the 'bird-hipped' Ornithischia. The Saurischians are sub-divided into theropods, who were carnivores and walked on their two hind limbs, and sauropods, who were four-legged plant-eaters. All the Ornithischians, sub-divided into ornithopods, ceratopsians, stegasaurs and ankylosaurs, were plant-eaters. The fossilised skeleton of an Iguanodon (an Ornithopod) was found at Hanover Point in 1972. An ancient fossil forest can also be seen here at low tide. Iguanadon could be 30 feet long and 18 feet high. They grazed in herds, like elephants.

Refreshments   Ice-cream vans may visit the car parks in summer.

Route 12

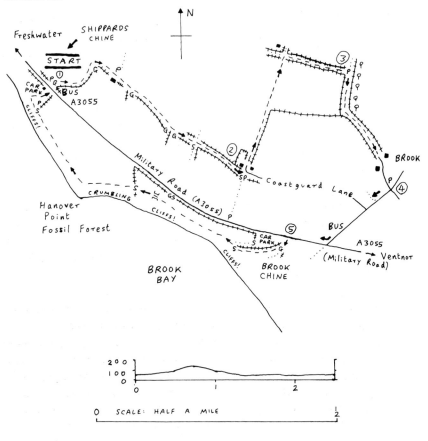

Freshwater

SHIPPARDS CHINE

START

N

CAR PARK
BUS
A3055

CLIFFS!

① G P

G P

S

G

G

Military Road (A3055)

CRUMBLING

CLIFFS!

S GS

Hanover Point
Fossil Forest

③ P

BROOK

Coastguard Lane

④ P

② SP

BUS

⑤

CAR PARK
S
G

BROOK BAY

CLIFFS!

BROOK CHINE

A3055
(Military Road)

Ventnor

200
100
0

0   1   2

0   SCALE: HALF A MILE   1/2

FEVERFEW white June - Sept.

54

Route 12

Brook Bay
2½ miles

START   *At the bus stop adjacent to the National Trust car park at Shippards Chine and Hanover Point. This is on the A3055 one mile west of Brook (G.R. 378841).*

ROUTE

1. *With your back to the car park, go left along the A3055 for 50 metres, with the sea on your left. Turn right through a gate along the signposted public footpath 57. Follow a track with a fence on your right. Pass a signposted path on your left and house (Compton Grange) on your right. Take public footpath BS87 ahead, towards Brook.*

2. *At the junction with the metalled Coastguard Lane, turn left along part of the Hamstead Trail (here path BS51). The lane soon turns into a rough track. Follow a hedge on your right then pass between open fields. Turn right at a crosstracks near a building.*

3. *Reach a signpost at a T-junction and turn right along path BS107 to Brook Village. This delivers you to Badger Lane.*

4. *Turn right at the crossroads in Brook. Ignore Carpenters Lane and Coastguard Lane on your right and pass the bus stop on your way to the A3055. Turn right along its grassy verge for about 250 metres.*

5. *Turn left to follow the Coastal Path from Brook Chine. There is a stile at the back of the car park, but if you go through the gate to the left of it and follow a fence on your right, there is another stile to bring you to the clifftop path. BEWARE! These cliffs are crumbling and could be dangerous, especially for unsupervised children. Follow the Coastal Path above Brook Bay on your left back to Shippards Chine.*

Public Transport   The bus stops at both Shippards Chine and Brook are served by bus No. 1B which runs between Ryde, Newport and Freshwater Bay.

MORRIS DANCERS AT GODSHILL

Godshill

Outline   The Griffin Inn, Godshill ~ Beech Copse ~ Sainham Farm ~ Foot of Gat Cliff ~ Sheepwash Lane ~ Church of the Lily Cross, Godshill ~ The Griffin Inn, Godshill.

Summary   Despite all the tourist trivia and 'ye olde tea shops', Godshill is still a special place with many attractions for the young and young-at-heart. This walk takes you to some fine woodland on the gradual climb to the foot of Gat Cliff, before returning along a quiet lane.

Attractions   High fences along this route indicate the presence of deer. Painted Lady butterflies may be seen near the precipitous face of Gat Cliff, formed from an outcrop of Upper Greensand. Beech Copse can boast sweet chestnut, hazel, sycamore, silver birch, ash, holly, spindle and beech trees. May is the month to come for the carpet of bluebells, while primroses, wild daffodils and wood anemones can also be seen in the Spring. Despite all this natural splendour, little feet will be aching to see the artificial wonders of Godshill, which can dig deep into the pocket-money.

One of the great joys of Godshill is to walk around its Model Village. This contains the picturesque group of thatched cottages through which runs the path to the church. This picture is on the front cover of the Ordnance Survey map of the Isle of Wight and must be one of the most famous in England. It's great fun to compare the model with the real thing, especially when they are photographed. The church is built on top of a hill (God's Hill) because of supernatural interference with building work at a lower site, with the stones being removed during the night to here. This must be an ancient holy spot, perhaps where leys cross. The druids may have even arranged the nocturnal transportation of the stones to ensure site continuity. It is known as the Church of the Lily Cross because of a unique (to Britain - a few survive on the continent) mural on the East wall of the South transept. The name may also refer to the fact that leys cross here. The mural dates from about 1450 and was discovered in the middle of the 19th century underneath lime-wash applied over it at the Reformation or during Cromwell's rule. Significantly (if it does stand where leys cross), the church's tower has often been struck by lightning. Outside stands a 15th century cross and an 18th century sundial.

Do pay your admission fees to see the Model Village. This contains a model of the model of the model. Shanklin is also here in miniature. The opening hours are 10 a.m. to 5 p.m. daily in April, May, June and

continued on page 60

Route 13

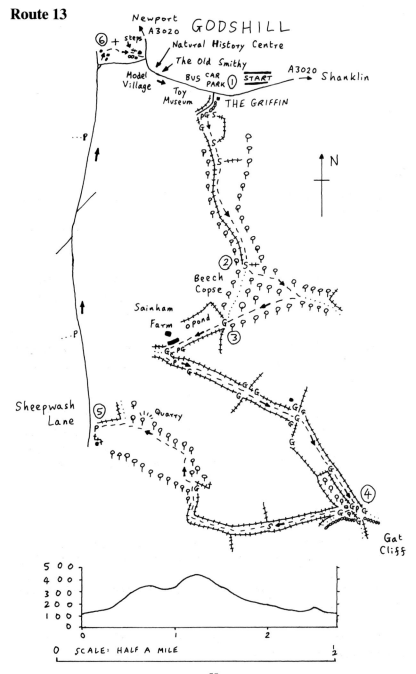

Route 13

Godshill

2¾ miles

START   *The Griffin Inn has a car park across the road and a bus stop nearby, so start from here on the A3020 as it leaves Godshill for Shanklin (G.R. 530817).*

ROUTE

1. *Face the Griffin and take the lane ahead on the right of it. Very soon, bear left over a stile beside a gate and follow the signposted path GL57 to Beech Copse. Keep beside the perimeter fence of woodland on your right.*

2. *Cross a stile to enter Beech Copse and follow the right of way through the trees which bears left to a path junction. Turn sharply right here to take this higher path to a gate at the edge of the copse.*

3. *Go ahead with a high deer fence on your left. Pass Sainham Farm and turn sharply left along the signposted public footpath GL58 towards Gatcliff.*

4. *At the foot of Gatcliff, turn right along the signposted path GL49. This goes to Stenbury Down, but you soon fork right from it to take path GL59. This enclosed path emerges in a field given to clay pigeon shooting. The right of way goes around the right hand edge of this field, past a quarry, to reach Sheepwash Lane.*

5. *Turn right along the lane back to Godshill.*

6. *When you reach the much photographed access between thatched cottages to Godshill Church (as on the cover of the O.S. Outdoor Leisure map 29), go up to the church. Continue, with the church on your left before descending along steps to the A3020 in Godshill. Go right back to the Griffin Inn.*

Public Transport Godshill is served by buses Nos. 2 (Sandown-Shanklin-Newport-Cowes) and 2A (Newport-Ventnor).

September. July and August brings an extension to 9 p.m. (5.30 p.m. on Saturdays), with illuminations from 7 p.m. It is open from 10.30 a.m. to 4 p.m. in October (to the last Friday).

Godshill has much else besides. The Old Smithy has an aviary and a model garden, while the Natural History Centre has an aquarium and a museum. A real delight is the Toy Museum, with a huge display of toys dating from 1945. All the famous names are here - Hornby, Matchbox, Dinky, Corgi, Triang, Britains . . . This is open daily between Easter and October (inclusive) from 10 a.m. to 5 p.m. (plus evenings in July and August).

Refreshments Plenty of choice in Godshill.

COTTAGES AT GODSHILL

The Ventnor Line

Outline Shanklin British Rail Station ~ Dismantled Railway ~ America Wood ~ Shanklin British Rail Station.

Summary The ghosts of old trains may be met on this walk. The old line towards Ventnor provides such easy walking that it would suit a moonlit night. You'll need sunlight to follow an attractive path through the trees in America Wood before taking fieldpaths back to Shanklin, with its caravan parks and holiday chalets.

Attractions Shanklin was a favourite resort of the American poet Henry Wadsworth Longfellow. Whilst in the resort, do visit Shanklin Chine. Chines are steepsided narrow gulleys along the coast, formed by the dual erosion of the sea wearing away the cliff face and downward erosion by streams and rivers into the cliff. John Keats stayed near Shanklin Chine and wished he had a penny for each visitor entering it. You'll pay more than one penny today! Longfellow wrote a poem after seeing it ('Traveller, stay thy weary feet'). It is open daily from Easter to mid October (9.30 a.m. to 5.30 p.m. in April and May, to 10 p.m. from June to September and to 4 p.m. in October).

Shanklin is fortunate to have retained its British Rail station. Always the most viable of the Island's railways, the line from Ryde Pier Head to Shanklin was saved after vigorous local protests. Dr. Beeching had his way with the extension to Ventnor, however, closing it on 18th April, 1966. Why, oh why? Poor Ventnor now suffers from the lack of a quick connection with the Portsmouth catamaran (it's only 22 minutes by electric train from Shanklin to Ryde Pier Head). The trains can also be used if you hold a Bus Rover (day, week or four week tickets available). Even the electric trains are of interest, having been built for the London Underground in 1938. British Rail have made such a good job of upgrading them that they don't seem so old. The railway first reached Shanklin from Ryde (St. John's Road initially) on 23rd August, 1864. The extension to Ventnor was opened on 15th September, 1866. It was forced to go through Wroxall by the local landowner, the Earl of Yarborough, and approached Ventnor through a tunnel under St. Boniface Down.

Refreshments America Cottages in America Wood, or in Shanklin.

Route 14

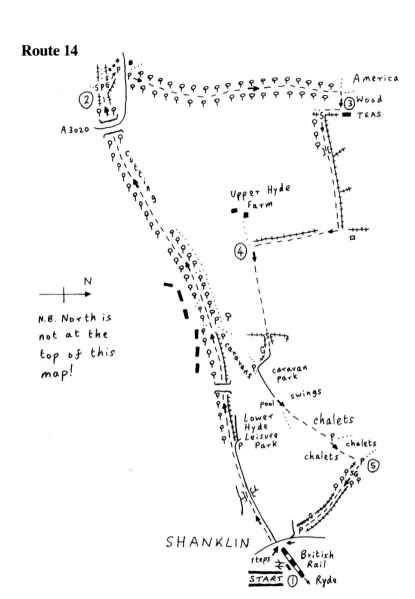

America
Wood
② TEAS
A 3020
③

Cutting

Upper Hyde
Farm
④

N

N.B. North is
not at the
top of this
map!

caravans

caravan
park

swings

pool

chalets

Lower
Hyde
Leisure
Park

chalets

chalets
⑤

SHANKLIN

steps
British
Rail
START ① Ryde

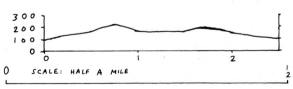

300
200
100
0

0   1   2

0   SCALE: HALF A MILE   1/2

Route 14
The Ventnor Line

2½ miles

START *Finding the start of this walk couldn't be easier - it begins at Shanklin's British Rail station (G.R. 581819).*

ROUTE

1. *The railway now terminates at Shanklin. Go down the steps south of the station, cross the road and walk beside a new road built on the trackbed of its former extension to Ventnor. There is a suburban feel at first, then the road enters Lower Hyde Leisure Park on your right. Go ahead along the path signposted to Wroxall set in the old railway cutting. This leads under an attractive bridge bearing the A3020. Open countryside follows, but you are about to leave the old line.*

2. *Turn right over a stile beside a gate and follow the signposted public footpath NC39 towards America Wood. Cross a road and veer right along a signposted woodland path, NC37a, towards Ninham. This, in fact, takes you to America Wood. Turn right when you reach a waymarked post at a crosspaths. This leads you to America Cottages, where refreshments are obtainable during the season.*

3. *Turn right to pass the cottages on your right. Turn left across a stile and walk with a fence on your left. Cross a tiny footbridge over a ditch at the edge of the wood and continue beside a hedge on your left and, perhaps, maize in the field on your right. Turn right after entering the next field, which may be full of cabbages.*

4. *Turn left along a grassy track between two open fields. Go ahead over a stile and follow a road into a caravan park. Continue along a track to pass swings on your left and a pool on your right. Descend past chalets to a signpost. Fork right past more chalets along path SS17 to Shanklin.*

5. *Turn right along the signposted bridleway SS18. Cross a stile beside a gate and follow the path up to a road. Go right to the station, which is up the steps on your left.*

Public Transport Enjoy a ride to Shanklin on the Island's electric trains, which connect with catamarans from Portsmouth at Ryde Pier Head. There are buses to Shanklin from Cowes (No. 2), Newport (Nos. 2, 16 and 16B), Ventnor (Nos. 16 and 16B), Sandown (Nos. 2, 8, 16 and 16B) and Ryde (Nos. 8, 16 and 16B).

BLACKGANG ATTRACTIONS

Blackgang

Outline   Blackgang Chine ~ St. Catherine's Oratory ~ Chale Farm ~ Blackgang Chine.

Summary   This is a strenuous walk, involving a climb to nearly 800 feet above sea level (from 400 feet). You won't be alone, however, as this is very popular with families and school parties. The reason is the strange 'pepperpot' on the top of St. Catherine's Hill. Come on a fine day for memorable views and allow time to visit Blackgang Chine.

Attractions   Visit Blackgang while it's still here! Every so often bits of it slip into the sea. This is only to be expected in a place that was cursed by the holy man from the oratory above it. He did this in response to the activities of the local giant, who was a cannibal. The sinister nature of the place is confirmed by tales of shipwrecks and smuggling. The views along this route are superb, however, while the top of St. Catherine's Hill obviously provides vision of a spiritual kind too.

Blackgang Chine is now more of a theme park than a chine, as at Shanklin, for example. First opened as a tourist attraction in 1843, it initially displayed the skeleton of a whale that had been stranded off the Needles in 1842. Now it features a model village, a gnome garden, a maze, water gardens, a Nurseryland complete with a fairy castle, dinosaur replicas, a scene from the American 'Wild West', Jungleland, and adventure playground and displays relevant to the local history of smuggling and lifeboats. Blackgang Chine is open daily from April to October between 10 a.m. and 5 p.m. (10 p.m. with illuminations from June to September).

The viewpoint from the car park near the A3055 provides a wonderful view of West Wight. The bays along the coast are spread out before you as if on a map. Chale Bay is the nearest, followed by Brighstone Bay, Brook Bay, Compton Bay and Freshwater Bay. Dorset is in the background. Dozens, if not hundreds, of ships have been wrecked here. In 1314, the Pope ordered the local landowner, Walter de Godeton, to build the 'pepperpot' on the summit of St. Catherine's Hill as a penance for plundering wine from the wreck of the 'St. Mary', a French ship. A lighthouse and chapel functioned here until the Reformation. Nearly 36 feet high, the oratory is a curious building with a pyramidal roof, eight sides outside and four inside. Leys can be shown to cross here (bring your dowsing rods) and one, curiously, continues over an ancient round barrow and the remains of a late tower (the 'mustard pot',

continued on page 68

65

Route 15

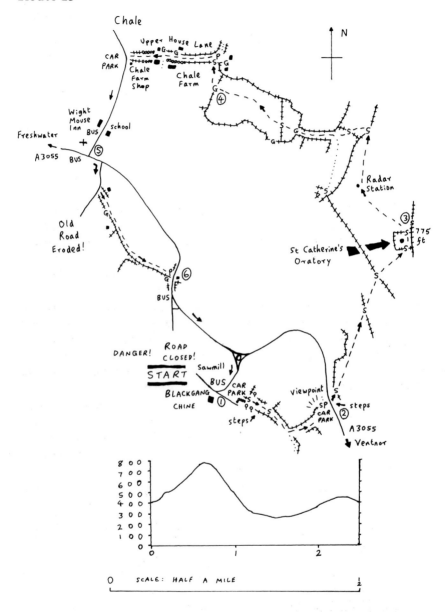

Chale

Upper House Lane

CAR PARK

G   G   P

Chale Farm Shop

Chale Farm

G

④

Wight Mouse Inn

BUS   school

Freshwater

A3055   BUS   ⑤

G

Old Road Eroded!

G

P   ⑥

BUS

Radar Station

③   775 ft

St Catherine's Oratory

S

DANGER!   ROAD CLOSED!

START

BLACKGANG CHINE   ①

BUS   CAR PARK

Sawmill

steps

Viewpoint

SP CAR PARK   ②   steps

A3055

Ventnor

N

800
700
600
500
400
300
200
100
0

0   1   2

0   SCALE: HALF A MILE   ½

Route 15

Blackgang

2½ miles

START   *The giant figure of a smuggler stands with legs astride outside the entrance to Blackgang Chine. A bus stop is nearby, as is a car park (G.R. 488768).*

ROUTE

1. *With your back to the entrance of Blackgang Chine, go right to pass the Ship Ashore Inn and turn left, then right into the car park. Take the steps in the corner to go ahead over a stile and up more steps. Continue past a grassy area on your left and up more steps ahead. Reach the clifftop, where the sea is on your right. Turn left along a path which goes inland to a viewpoint and a car park beside the A3055.*

2. *Go ahead up steps on the far side of the road. Cross a stile to enter a sloping pasture and walk near a fence on your left. When it bears left, keep climbing to a stile in the fence ahead. Cross it to continue to and over another stile in a higher fence. Go ahead to the distinctive 'pepperpot' of St. Catherine's Oratory on the 775 ft. summit of this grassy hill.*

3. *Bear left as you descend to pass a radar station and veer right from it to reach a stile in a fence. Cross this to bear left down a steep slope along a path between blackberry bushes. Cross a stile on your left at the foot of the slope and go right along a fenced path to a fieldgate. Go ahead along a path across a field, soon crossing a stile in a fence ahead. Continue to the gate at the far end of the field.*

4. *Go through the gate and turn right to a stile. Cross this to reach a lane, and go left along it to a road. Turn left, past Chale Farm Shop (children welcome) on your left, then the Wight Mouse Inn (children welcome) on your right. Reach the junction with the A3055, with Chale's St. Andrew's Church on your right.*

5. *Turn left along the A3055 briefly, then take the first turning on your right. This old road is being eroded by the sea, but you soon turn left off it along public bridleway C15 (Coastal Path to Blackgang). Keep a fence on your right and pass more blackberries on your left. Return to the A3055 at a signpost and near a bus stop.*

6. *Go right and fork left along the A3055 (the road forking right is closed because of the danger of subsidence). Take the new access road down to the entrance of Blackgang Chine on your right.*

Public Transport   Blackgang Chine is served by bus No. 16 (Newport-Ryde via Shanklin and Sandown).

abandoned in 1785 as fog obscured its light) to reach the sea at Reeth Bay. Reeth is derived from wraith, referring to the ghosts of drowned sailors. Leys appear to be spirit paths used by the souls of the dead, while they are also associated with lights in the sky similar to the 'wheels' named after St. Catherine. Puckaster, near Reeth Bay, may once have been the country's major tin port. If so, Joseph of Arimathea probably brought the young Jesus here. The summit of St. Catherine's Hill seems to have had a hermitage in ancient times.

The current lighthouse was built in 1840 at the foot of the cliff at only 72 feet above sea level (to overcome the problem of hill fog). It was built after the loss of the 'Clarendon' in 1836. One of the bodies of those drowned (a Miss Gourley) was swept by the sea to the foot of her father's garden - in Southsea, on the mainland. Another strange coincidence was that one of the rescued men had previously saved the life of his rescuer, on another ship. Most of those who died in the wreck of the 'Clarendon' are buried in Chale Church.

Refreshments   At Blackgang Chine and in the Wight Mouse Inn, Chale. Children are also welcome at Chale Farm Shop.

Ventnor Botanic Garden

Outline   Ventnor Botanic Garden ~ Steephill Cove ~ Ventnor Botanic Garden.

Summary   This short walk could take all day. The Garden is open every day and admission is free.

Attractions   Ventnor Botanic Garden's 22 acres enjoy a mild climate and a southerly aspect on the famous 'Undercliff'. This coastal area has been subject to landslips in the past. These have been produced by porous chalk and upper greensands rocks lying on top of gault clay (known locally as the 'blue slipper'). There are curved rupture surfaces within the gault clay and movement is liable to occur when this becomes lubricated by water percolating down from the surface. The rupture or slip surface allows the rocks to move seawards. At the same time, the curved surface rotates the layering in the rocks so that it tilts steeply inland. Sandwiched between the sea and the steeply rising downs, the Undercliff has its own very localised climate. It is very sheltered, making winters warmer. Sea mists are common, with moisture condensing from onshore breezes forced to rise over the downs. This encourages plant growth and the impression of a jungle of oak trees on a carpet of ferns is easily forged. The early visitors admired this picturesque scenery, while Ventnor became famous as a winter resort. The Royal National Hospital for Diseases of the Chest was erected here in 1868. Patients were encouraged to work outside in the gardens and they were sent hundreds of bulbs to plant by Covent Garden.

When the hospital was demolished in the 1960s (its site is now the car park), its grounds were saved to form this Botanic Garden. Sir Harold Hillier, the internationally famous plantsman from Winchester, masterminded its establishment in 1969. He donated hundreds of shrubs, including many from New Zealand, which enjoy the local Maritime Mediterranean climate with its lack of frosts. The Botanic Garden was officially opened to the public in 1972 by the then Governor of the Island, His Excellency Earl Mountbatten of Burma. Unfortunately, many of the exotic plants didn't survive the unexpectedly harsh winters of the early 1980s and over 300 mature trees were lost in the great storm of 16th October, 1987. There is still much to see, however. The plants are displayed according to themes. There is a wild meadow area, a palm garden and a New Zealand garden, while many plants are of historical, medical or culinary interest. Rock samphire, a low, bushy, plant with

continued on page 72

Route 16

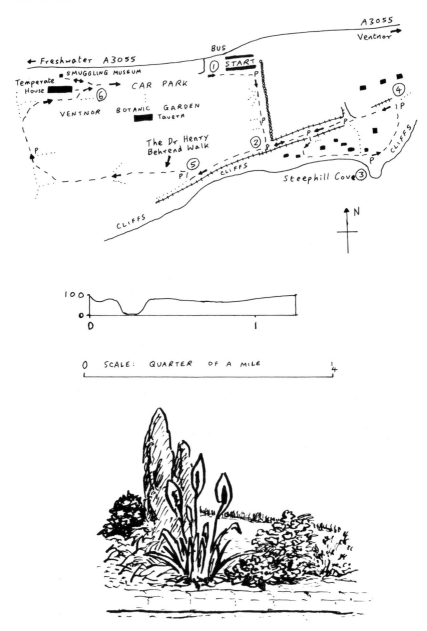

A3055
Ventnor

BUS

← Freshwater A3055
START

SMUGGLING MUSEUM

Temperate
House

CAR PARK

VENTNOR   BOTANIC   GARDEN
Tavern

The Dr Henry
Behrend Walk

Steephill Cove

CLIFFS

CLIFFS

CLIFFS

N

100

0

D   1

0   SCALE: QUARTER   OF   A   MILE   ¼

Route 16

Ventnor Botanic Garden   1¼ miles

START   *The entrance to Ventnor Botanic Garden. There is a bus stop near it, on the A3055 one mile west of Ventnor. There is a large car park here (G.R. 548770).*

ROUTE

1. *From the entrance, go left to the eastern end of the car park. Turn right to follow the signposted path towards the coast, walking with the Garden's perimeter wall on your left.*

2. *Turn left along the signposted Coastal Path. Take the first signposted path on your right. This descends steeply to the beach at Steephill Cove. Go left with the sea on your right, passing picturesque cottages on your left.*

3. *Go ahead along the signposted Coastal Path towards Ventnor. This gradually climbs to rejoin the clifftop path at a signpost.*

4. *Turn left along the clifftop path to walk with the sea now on your left. Ignore the access road on your right and a signposted path back down to Steephill Cove on your left. Take path V90 ahead towards St. Lawrence.*

5. *Fork right into the Botanic Garden to follow the Dr. Henry Behrend Walk. Fork right again as you approach the perimeter wall and reach another signpost. Go ahead with the wall on your left up to the Temperate House.*

6. *Divert left to visit the Smuggling Museum before walking the length of the car park back to the entrance.*

Public Transport   Bus No. 16B (Ryde-Newport via Shanklin) serves the entrance to Ventnor Botanic Garden.

yellow umbels can be seen on an exposed cliff. The small white flowers of feverfew can be seen on the seaward side of the dry stone wall which separates the meadow from the recreation green above.

The Temperate House was completed in 1987 and provides an environment in which plants from the warm temperate zones of the world can thrive and be protected from frost. This is where you can now find the plants replacing those lost, from Australia, South African and South America, plus some from the Canary Islands and the Azores. Look out for eucalyptus trees and a dragon tree. A red gum from this was prized by medieval alchemists. There are also unique plants from the remote South Atlantic island of St. Helena. Many of the plants here are threatened with extinction in the wild. There is a small admission fee to see the Temperate House, which is open daily (10 a.m.-5 p.m. from Easter to October, 11 a.m.-3 p.m. on winter weekdays and 1 p.m.-4 p.m. on winter Sundays).

When the hospital was pulled down, its vaults and cellars were left intact. Extending under the A3055, these now house the colourful tableaux of the Museum of Smuggling History. The admission charge is well worth paying to see the fascinating display of smuggling methods, dating back to the 13th century wool trade. As Rudyard Kipling wrote:

'Them that asks no questions isn't told a lie.
Watch the wall, my darling, while the gentlemen go by!
Five and twenty ponies
Trotting through the dark -
Brandy for the Parson,
'Baccy for the Clerk;
Laces for a lady, letters for a spy,
Watch the wall, my darling, while the gentlemen go by!'

The Museum of Smuggling History is open daily from Easter to September between 9 a.m. and 5 p.m.

Steephill Cove is a magical little bay, hidden away from all but Coastal Path walkers. Come here to sunbathe and watch the foam hit the rocks.

Refreshments   Ventnor Botanic Garden has a tavern. This is open daily and on summer evenings. There is also a cafe serving freshly-caught seafood in Steephill Cove.

Appendices

Approximate mileage of each walk from Yarmouth, Newport and Ryde via main roads.

Route	Yarmouth	Newport	Ryde
1	13	5	8
2	1	11	19
3	0	10	18
4	9	1	9
5	14	4	4
6	4	12	20
7	3	11	19
8	3	11	19
9	6	6	14
10	13	3	7
11	18	8	5
12	6	9	17
13	16	6	12
14	20	10	9
15	14	10	18
16	19	12	13

CANNON AT CARISBROOKE

ROUTES IN ORDER OF DIFFICULTY

None of these walks would be strenuous to an experienced walker. The following grading is made in the context of a Family Walks book and is done with the fairly active six or seven year old in mind.

Easy Walks

Route 1 - *Cowes (3¼ miles)*
Route 2 - *Fort Victoria (2½ miles)*
Route 3 - *St. Swithin's Church (3 miles)*
Route 12 - *Brook Bay (2½ miles)*
Route 14 - *The Ventnor Line (2½ miles)*

Moderately Difficult

Route 5 - *Havenstreet (3½ miles)*
Route 6 - *Alum Bay (3 miles)*
Route 9 - *Calbourne Mill (3 miles)*
Route 16 - *Ventnor Botanic Garden (1¼ miles)*

More Strenuous

Route 4 - *Carisbrooke Castle (2 miles)*
Route 7 - *Tennyson Down (3 miles)*
Route 8 - *Afton Down (2½ miles)*
Route 10 - *Arreton Manor (3¼ miles)*
Route 11 - *Morton Manor (3¼ miles)*
Route 13 - *Godshill (2¾ miles)*
Route 15 - *Blackgang (2½ miles)*

ROCK SAMPHIRE yellow July - Oct.

PUBLIC TRANSPORT

The Isle of Wight is an ideal place for using public transport. It is also not the sort of place that should be polluted by more private cars. If you have a car, leave it at home and buy a foot passenger ticket on one of the several forms of ferry across the Solent. British Rail can take you to Lymington for the ferry to Yarmouth, or to Portsmouth Harbour for the catamaran for Ryde Pier Head. A special bus service takes passengers between the port and the railway station in Southampton, from where you can take a hydrofoil to Cowes. On the Island, buy the local bus timetable and Southern Vectis Bus/Rail Rovers. These tickets can be bought for a day, a week or for four weeks and offer excellent value, as well as flexibility. Full details are available from:

The Southern Vectis Omnibus Co. Ltd., Head Office, Nelson Road, Newport, Isle of Wight, PO30 1RD. Tel. 0983 522456.

MODEL VILLAGE AT GODSHILL

75

TOURIST INFORMATION ADDRESSES

The Isle of Wight Tourist Office, Quay Store, Town Quay, Newport, Isle of Wight, PO30 2EF. Tel. 0983 524343. There are seasonal Tourist Information Centres at Cowes, Newport, Ryde, Ventnor and Yarmouth, while the Tourist Information Centres at Sandown and Shanklin remain open all year.

WET WEATHER ALTERNATIVES. Completely or partly under cover.
The Isle of Wight is so small and the bus/rail rover so flexible that anywhere on the Island could be considered as an alternative for any particular walk. The following list is far from being comprehensive!

Walk 1:	Cowes Toy and Model Museum and the Isle of Wight Model Railway.
Walk 2:	Fort Victoria Museum and Aquarium, Golden Hill Fort.
Walk 3:	Yarmouth Castle, Lymington Ferry.
Walk 4:	Carisbrooke Castle, Newport Roman Villa and Pirates' Ship.
Walk 5:	Isle of Wight Steam Railway and Brickfields Horsecountry.
Walk 6:	Needles Pleasure Park, Alum Bay Glass and Needles Old Battery.
Walk 7:	As for route 6.
Walk 8:	Freshwater Redoubt.
Walk 9:	Calbourne Mill.
Walk 10:	Arreton Manor, Arreton Craft Village, Robin Hill and Haseley Manor.
Walk 11:	Morton Manor, Brading Wax Museum, Brading Roman Villa and Brading Dolls Museum.
Walk 12:	Chessell Porcelain and Isle of Wight Pearl.
Walk 13:	Godshill Model Village, Toy Museum, Old Smithy and Natural History Centre.
Walk 14:	Shanklin Chine, British Rail's Island Line and Sandown Geology Museum.
Walk 15:	Blackgang Chine.
Walk 16:	Ventnor Botanic Garden and Museum of Smuggling History.

Step right in to this old rock.
Rest chin on wall below the Block.
Tilt head on side. lopsided grin
Tongue outstretched and eyes turned in.
Compose yourself whilst cameras measure
This happy snap for all to treasure.

DON'T LOSE YOUR HEAD! BRADING WAX MUSEUM

77

FAMILY WALKS SERIES

Family Walks in the North Yorkshire Dales. Howard Beck. ISBN 0 907758 52 5.

Family Walks in West Yorkshire. Howard Beck. ISBN 0 907758 43 6.

Family Walks in Three Peaks and Malham. Howard Beck. ISBN 0 907758 42 8.

Family Walks in South Yorkshire. Norman Taylor. ISBN 0 907758 25 8.

Family Walks in the North Wales Borderlands. Gordon Emery. ISBN 0 907758 50 9.

Family Walks in Cheshire. Chris Buckland. ISBN 0 907758 29 0.

Family Walks in the Staffordshire Peak and Potteries. Les Lumsdon. ISBN 0 907758 34 7.

Family Walks in the White Peak. Norman Taylor. ISBN 0 907758 09 6.

Family Walks in the Dark Peak. Norman Taylor. ISBN 0 907758 16 9.

Family Walks in Snowdonia. Laurence Main. ISBN 0 907758 32 0.

Family Walks in Mid Wales. Laurence Main. ISBN 0 907758 27 4.

Family Walks in South Shropshire. Marian Newton. ISBN 0 907758 30 4.

Family Walks in the Teme Valley. Camilla Harrison. ISBN 0 907758 45 2.

Family Walks in Hereford and Worcester. Gordon Ottewell. ISBN 0 907758 20 7.

Family Walks around Cardiff and the Valleys. Gordon Hindess. ISBN 0 907758 54 1.

Family Walks in the Wye Valley. Heather and Jon Hurley. ISBN 0 907758 26 6.

Family Walks in Warwickshire. Geoff Allen. ISBN 0 907758 53 3.

Family Walks around Stratford and Banbury. Gordon Ottewell. ISBN 0 907758 49 5.

Family Walks in the Cotswolds. Gordon Ottewell. ISBN 0 907758 15 0.

Family Walks in South Gloucestershire. Gordon Ottewell. ISBN 0 907758 33 9.

Family Walks in Oxfordshire. Laurence Main. ISBN 0 907758 38 X.

Family Walks around Bristol, Bath and the Mendips. Nigel Vile. ISBN 0 907758 19 3.

Family Walks in Wiltshire. Nigel Vile. ISBN 0 907758 21 5.

Family Walks in Berkshire and North Hampshire. Kathy Sharp. ISBN 0 907758 37 1.

Family Walks on Exmoor and the Quantocks. John Caswell. ISBN 0 907758 46 0.

Family Walks in Mendip, Avalon and Sedgemoor. Nigel Vile. ISBN 0 907758 41 X.

Family Walks in Cornwall. John Caswell. ISBN 0 907758 55 X.

Family Walks on the Isle of Wight. Laurence Main. ISBN 0 907758 56 8.

Family Walks in North West Kent. Clive Cutter. ISBN 0 907758 36 3.

Family Walks in the Weald of Kent and Sussex. Clive and Sally Cutter. ISBN 0 907758 51 7.

The Publishers, D. J. Mitchell and E. G. Power welcome suggestions for further titles in this Series; and will be pleased to consider manuscripts relating to Derbyshire from new or established authors.
